4 22

~~Bishop~~
T. L. Rowland

Chad
Heatwole

New BEGINNINGS

Real Stories
from Zanesville, Ohio

Copyright © 2014 Good Catch Publishing, Beaverton, OR.

All rights reserved. Written permission must be secured from the publisher to use or reproduce any part of this book, except for brief quotations in critical reviews or articles.

This book was written for the express purpose of conveying the love and mercy of Jesus Christ. The statements in this book are substantially true; however, names and minor details have been changed to protect people and situations from accusation or incrimination.

All Scripture quotations, unless otherwise noted, are taken from the New International Version Copyright 1973, 1984, 1987 by International Bible Society.

Published in Beaverton, Oregon, by Good Catch Publishing.
www.goodcatchpublishing.com
V1.1

Printed in the United States of America

Table of Contents

	Dedication	9
	Acknowledgements	11
	Introduction	15
1	Hand On My Shoulder	17
2	A Mother's Plea	45
3	Home Sweet Home	73
4	Out of Death	97
5	Houses, Home and Harmony	135
6	The One	171
7	Speechless	191
	Conclusion	221

DEDICATION

This book is dedicated to all those who've struggled
and made a new beginning, and to all those whose life
is a mess right now and who yearn to believe
a new beginning is possible.

ACKNOWLEDGEMENTS

I would like to thank Terry Rowland for his vision for this book and Heidi Wells for her hard work in making it a reality.

To the people of TFG, thank you for your boldness and vulnerability in sharing your personal stories.

This book would not have been published without the amazing efforts of our project manager and editor, Hayley Pandolph. Her untiring resolve pushed this project forward and turned it into a stunning victory. Thank you for your great fortitude and diligence. Deep thanks to our incredible editor in chief, Michelle Cuthrell, and executive editor, Jen Genovesi, for all the amazing work they do. I would also like to thank our invaluable proofreader, Melody Davis, for the focus and energy she has put into perfecting our words.

Lastly, I want to extend our gratitude to the creative and very talented Jenny Randle, who designed the beautiful cover for *New Beginnings: Real Stories from Zanesville, Ohio.*

Daren Lindley
President and CEO
Good Catch Publishing

The book you are about to read
is a compilation of authentic life stories.
The facts are true, and the events are real.
These storytellers have dealt with crisis, tragedy, abuse
and neglect and have shared their most private moments,
mess-ups and hang-ups in order for others to learn and
grow from them. In order to protect the identities of those
involved in their pasts, the names and details of some
storytellers have been withheld or changed.

INTRODUCTION

Life can go wrong in so many ways. You may be wondering if it's even possible to start fresh. Can someone make a new beginning after years of bad decisions? After the death of a child? After pain, disappointment, struggle or despair?

As the true stories in this book demonstrate, YES! There is hope! New beginnings are possible, and they're possible for you. Journey with seven real people from right here in Zanesville, Ohio, as they share their heartbreaks and hardships — and how they found the strength to move beyond its grip on their lives, and how you can, too.

HAND ON MY SHOULDER
The Story of Richard
Written by Douglas Abbott

I was dying. It was official: The doctor said I had four months to live. The disease had taken more than 60 pounds off my frame and stolen all the strength in my body. I had almost completely lost my mobility. Soon, they would put me in a pine box, lower me into the ground and say asinine things over my grave.

I refused to allow myself to be concerned about my illness. It was just the latest in a string of impersonal atrocities I had endured. Life had done nothing for me if it hadn't taught me to expect just such things from it. One more blow couldn't make much of a difference.

Even if it was the last one.

☙☙☙

I grew up in a stable, loving military family in Roseville, Ohio. We lived in a mobile home on my grandparents' farm where we tended livestock and grew our own produce.

My mother was a quiet, steady presence in the house, always cooking and cleaning whenever she wasn't at work. We never lacked for anything.

I had two older sisters from Mom's previous marriage, Karen and Adrianne. We all lived together free from strife.

New BEGINNINGS

My father told us constantly how much he loved us. Whenever we wanted to go fishing or exploring with him, he made time to take us. The wide-open spaces in our backyard provided the perfect environment for camping, fishing and hunting. Dad also was a handyman. He could fix anything and was always showing me how to do framing, sheetrock, plumbing, auto mechanics and all kinds of household repairs. I kept busy helping my father fix vehicles and gadgets around the farm and building all kinds of things. I helped him build an addition onto our mobile home so my sisters could have their own rooms. He loved my sisters as though they were his own.

My maternal grandmother (we called her "Grandma S") was a great woman. However, all I remember was the regularity with which she sent me off to cut switches from a snowball bush for her to thrash me with, usually for small infractions. I got extra licks if it wasn't just the right weight and thickness. If procuring a switch was too time-consuming, Grandma S would simply lift me off the ground by my hair and punch me in the face.

My father often found fault with her for her harshness. However, in a big way, it was Grandma S who toughened me up for adulthood.

ಞಞಞ

When I was 10 years old, my father made an awful announcement.

"Your mother and I are getting a divorce."

HAND ON MY SHOULDER

I was speechless. I had never seen my parents fight. There had been no sign of strain, adultery or anything else I could imagine that might have broken their marriage.

And yet it happened. I felt an incredible sadness as I watched Dad drive away. He had been in the middle of everything I enjoyed. I felt like my life was coming to an end.

Not long after the divorce, my father re-enlisted in the Army. That meant I could only see him sporadically, when his schedule permitted him to drive out to see us. However, I spoke with him often over the phone.

After Grandma S died, Mom sold our trailer, and we moved into the farmhouse with Grandpa S. He took up with a girlfriend, but otherwise, everything continued as it had for many years. Grandpa S played banjo, mouth harp, spoons and a smattering of other instruments. It wasn't unusual to hear him singing and playing up a storm as I kicked around the farm. The whole family on my mother's side was musical. Before Grandma S died, they had a band and toured the region performing country music. Later, the remaining active members played at square dances. One of my strongest, purest memories is of hearing them play on the farm.

ॐॐॐ

My mother remarried when I was 12. My new stepfather, Don, came to live with us on the farm not long before Grandpa S died.

New BEGINNINGS

He was a decent man, hardworking — and an alcoholic, though it never kept him from fulfilling his family and work obligations.

Don loved beer, and since he never had much money, he had learned to brew and bottle his own. I tasted my first beer from Don's own supply on a hot summer day, and I loved it from the first sip. It had a sharp, snappy flavor and cooled my throat as the barley and hops bounced around in my mouth. I thought I had discovered the secret to peace and happiness as the alcohol made everything mellow. Very soon, I took an interest in learning how to brew it, which Don gladly showed me.

I had long enjoyed working with machines, and brewing beer was no different. We used a small furnace with a 55-gallon drum on each side. We organized crates full of bottles and a machine to cap them. After a batch was finished, the bottles would be placed in the root cellar.

The root cellar became my new favorite place to hang out. I sat for hours working with my chemistry set and drinking beer. I drank every evening without fail, though not heavily. However, as soon as summer came, whenever I wasn't working in the garden, I loaded a backpack full of beer and ventured into the woods next to our property. My family got used to my regular absences, some of which lasted for days.

For all practical purposes, I was a loner. Then Mom gave birth to my half-sister, Amanda Sue. Mandy thought I was the best thing since sliced bread and spent all her time following me around. I didn't care to have people

HAND ON MY SHOULDER

around most of the time, but I gladly made an exception for Mandy. Something about her personality soothed me. We played and explored together all over the farm and beyond. When she was only 5, I bought her a little Suzuki motorbike, which she was riding in no time.

Other than spending time with Mandy, my favorite activity was football. It was the only release valve I had found for my anger, which wasn't directed at people, but at life in general. I never stopped to analyze it, but it was there, smoldering just under the surface. The world that took my father from me had already been tried and convicted in my mind.

When I was a junior in high school, I asked Dad if I could live with him. He agreed, and I promptly moved to Aberdeen, Maryland. Before I left, I sat Mandy down and told her. I don't think she understood what was happening (she was still only 5), but my heart was breaking.

Dad lived in a mid-sized apartment just off the Army base. After I settled in, I enrolled in school and then turned my sights on the military culture there. I was fascinated by the marches, the exercises, the uniforms and the whole military tradition. Some evenings and weekends I would load up on beer and sneak onto the "Proving Grounds" at the post to watch the tank exercises. They would bury the tanks, winch them out and do it all over again. Sometimes I drank beer until I passed out. Later, I would wake up in the dark and go home.

Dad and I rebuilt several vehicles together while I lived with him. We made a pact that all our restoration projects

New BEGINNINGS

would be done together. We ended up with a whole collection of restored cars.

When I had been in Aberdeen for one year, Dad broke the news to me.

"I'm shipping off to Germany," he said without preamble.

I was excited. "That's awesome, Dad! You know I've had two years of German, right? Can I come?"

He didn't answer at first, and my heart sank.

"Dad, I want to go with you!"

He drew in a deep breath and let it out slowly. "I know. But you can't."

"Why not?"

"Your mother would be crushed. She doesn't want you traipsing around Europe."

My father had never lied to me, and I wanted to take him at his word. However, I had a strange feeling that maybe, instead, he wanted to get away from me.

We sold all the vehicles we had restored except the van, which he gave to me, along with some of the proceeds from the sales of the other cars. As Dad prepared to leave, I made plans of my own. I didn't want to go home. I had all I needed — a pocket full of money, three coolers full of beer and whiskey, a sleeping bag and a van to sleep in.

For some reason, I left before my father had finished wrapping up his affairs on the base. I was already starting to feel smothered in Aberdeen. There is a desolate feeling that comes with being in a place from which everyone is moving on. I wanted no part of it. I left a note for my father on the dining room table and lit out in the middle of the night.

> Dad,
>
> I'm heading out now. I'm going to travel around a bit, but I'll be back to the farm soon. I've had such a great time this past year. I hope you enjoy your stint in Germany. I love you.
>
> Richard

However, I didn't go back to the farm. The idea of being back there was somehow unsavory. It felt like a demotion. So I just decided to drive around the East Coast for a while. I called my father just before I knew he had to leave.

"Son, I'm a little put out with you. I thought we agreed you'd go back home."

"I will. I'm just doing some sightseeing first."

"Your mother's worried sick about you. Why don't you just go home?"

"I don't want to go back immediately. I promise I'll get back there before school starts."

Not long after I returned home, Mom and Don divorced. I didn't have a clue as to why, and at the time, I didn't care. I was becoming desensitized to upheaval.

I began to contemplate a career in the military. I had learned to love the military life, its traditions, the variety of different cultures and ethnicities, all bound together by a

New BEGINNINGS

strong military machine. Most of all, it was the life my father had chosen, and he was my idol.

My mother had different ideas.

"Please don't go join the military, Rick," she exhorted me.

"Why not?" I asked.

But she didn't give me a clear answer. All I knew was that she was dead-set against it. So I abandoned my plans.

I enrolled in my senior year almost reluctantly. However, my attitude changed after I met Adrianne's boyfriend, Joe. He was a weightlifter and the vice principal at the school. I was intrigued by him. He was different. He was like a big kid. He loved life and was never above goofing off when he wasn't doing his job. And yet he was an educated man who took his career seriously.

Joe turned me on to weightlifting. We started working out together constantly. I became quite strong and muscular. Over the course of that year, Joe and I traveled all over the East Coast competing in various tournaments. Because of his influence in my life, my drinking slowed down considerably.

❧❧❧

Because of my academic and athletic performance in high school, I was offered a scholarship to play football at Ohio University. However, I wasn't much interested in college. Mom had poured cold water on my military ambitions, and nothing else had any attraction for me.

HAND ON MY SHOULDER

Nevertheless, I went — with so little enthusiasm that it was almost a non-event. I traveled to Athens, Ohio, and took up residence in the dormitory housing. I rarely attended classes and even stopped showing up for football practice after a few sessions. My academic work was half-rate. To make matters worse, I took up drinking again and even took a job as a bouncer in a bar I frequented. Not only did I fit in with the crowd, I made a perfect bouncer: I was large and muscular and projected a smoldering anger. In my mind, the job gave me the freedom to hurt people without consequences. It was like football with fewer rules.

It didn't occur to me that I was headed down a dangerous road. A person cannot embrace life and burn with anger at the same time. I chose anger.

My schooling fizzled out before the end of the second quarter. I returned home clothed in a self-defeating apathy I didn't bother to examine. However, not long after my arrival home, Mom helped me land a job in a local pottery shop. The job gave me a resurgence of energy and enthusiasm. I had always loved working with my hands and learning new industrial skills. I avidly turned my attention to the work and to mastering the machinery. My job was to maintain the "train cars" that carried the flower pots and vases through the kiln — a job that made use of the welding skills Dad had taught me. I also kept the plate machine and the product dollies intact. Soon, I had learned the entire process from start to finish and could do anything in the shop, including fashioning the steel reinforcements for the product molds, which had to be

New BEGINNINGS

made with specific tolerances. I had found something I both enjoyed and excelled at.

Doing industrial work proved to be a "reset" for me. Before long, I was accepted as an apprentice electrical worker for a huge company. I was enjoying myself so much, I hardly flinched at the four years and 8,000 hours I would have to put in before I became a journeyman.

I was enjoying an after-work beer one evening when I met a short, beautiful girl named Charla in my favorite bar. She was gorgeous, engaging and enormously entertaining to be with. Hanging out with her was fun and completely effortless. We both enjoyed drinking beer and began seeing each other regularly. I fell for her in just a handful of weeks, and we married 10 months later. I bought an old mobile home, had it towed to Mom's farm and remodeled it from top to bottom. We were settling into our new home nicely when Mom knocked on our door one morning.

"Your father is ill," Mom said, after the three of us had sat down in the living room.

"Ill?"

"It's lung cancer. It's all through his body."

I was stunned. My father was my hero, a friend to dozens, the brightest spot in my memories and an unbreakable soldier. Now he was wasting away in a hospital bed, his throat burned from the radiation, his back one solid scab from the bedsores. I was heartbroken.

Charla and I drove out to Fort Wayne, Indiana, to see him as often as we could manage. The trips were unbearable. Seeing my father shrink toward death clashed horribly with my mind's image of his former strength. As we sat visiting with him, he spoke to us about God at a pace that seemed to accelerate as his sickness progressed.

Dad had been raised by Grandpa Norley, a Methodist preacher and an Army chaplain during World War II. Dad had brought me to services regularly during my upbringing. All my life, he had spoken of his faith in God, but now his words rang with growing intensity as he approached death. At the end of his horrific illness, while Charla and I looked on, my father sat up in bed, his arms stretched toward the ceiling, smiled from ear to ear and collapsed, dead.

I was destroyed. My aunts and uncles smiled and uttered what sounded to me like saccharine clichés about how Dad was no longer in pain but was now in the presence of God. All I could see was a good man, who had given generously to everyone, whom God had allowed to perish in awful pain. Anger rose up inside me, together with an utter contempt for God, the world and life itself.

Charla and I drank, fought and argued all the way home.

If I was a loner before, I was doubly one now, though I continued caring for Charla. I viewed the rest of the world with disdain. "You make what you have, and you survive," became my creed.

☙☙☙

New BEGINNINGS

Somehow, I shook off my grief over Dad's death and moved on. However, I was not the same man. I had become a self-proclaimed atheist. The only good things I acknowledged in life were my wife, Charla, and my work, which gave me a private corner in the world that I scarcely enjoyed.

After four years of study and meticulous work, I became a journeyman electrician earning a considerable wage. Leisure for me was drinking hard in local bars, where my hair-trigger temper often got me into fistfights. It wasn't unusual for me to spend a night in jail for assault.

I had given up on all my ideals, but I still carried two principles my father had imparted to me: *Family is everything*, and *If you say you're going to do something, you do it*.

Charla developed a cyst. Neither of us had an inkling how serious it was, but we found out after it burst, sending her to the ER, where she underwent emergency surgery. I discovered afterward that she'd had a hysterectomy.

I had longed passionately to have children. I tried to relieve my multiplying anger by working harder and longer.

Charla descended into a deep depression and drank constantly. Then the unthinkable occurred when Charla became unfaithful to me. Surely it was more a product of her depression and drunkenness than anything else, but it was more than I could take. In a mad rage, I tracked down the man, broke his door down and beat him severely. After the police came, he was taken to the hospital in an ambulance, and I was taken to jail, where I spent three days for assault.

Strangely, none of these events caused me to seriously examine the course I was on. My response was to grow angrier and more hateful toward the world and to work harder. It didn't help that bills from my father's hospitalization were overwhelming us financially. I could have simply allowed his estate to declare bankruptcy, but I refused to tarnish my father's legacy. I resolved to pay every dime that was owed to the hospitals, doctors and probate lawyers.

I landed a gig at a nuclear power plant in Oswego, New York. After proving myself, I was promoted and thereafter worked seven days a week, 12 to 16 hours per day on a wire-pulling crew. I still don't know how I managed to keep it up for eight and a half months. I was like the walking dead. After the job finished, I returned home, comforted in the knowledge that Dad's bills were all paid.

Years of turmoil and heavy drinking had taken their toll on Charla, who also was diagnosed with bipolar disorder and schizophrenia and continued to unravel mentally. She often stayed away from home for days at a time and began sliding in and out of psychiatric hospitals and alcohol treatment centers.

Around this time, my boss, Randy, brought me into his office.

"Rick, I'm concerned about you. You seem to have trouble working with others. I have no problem with what

New BEGINNINGS

you do on your own time as long as it doesn't affect your work. The fact is, you're drinking too much."

I sat there looking at him for a few seconds. "No problem. I don't need it. I've only been using it to help me cope with everything that's been going on, especially my wife's problems. That's okay. I'll quit."

So I did. Over the next two days, I began to sweat profusely and experienced uncontrollable anger and severe anxiety. My hands shook terribly. After a while, I took a few shots of Jim Beam and felt better.

The next day, Randy approached me around midday.

"How are things going, Rick?"

I exploded. "It's none of your business! You know what? My wife's at home screwing around on me. I don't need your attitude!" And I walked out.

I had never quit a job in my life. All the way home, I heard Dad's voice in my head. I had sorely disappointed him. The fact that he was no longer here made it worse.

I expressed my self-loathing by going on a three-day drunk. I ricocheted from bar to bar, cursing my existence.

When I got home, Charla and I began fighting immediately. I don't even recall the issues, let alone the words. We were both messed up, but Charla was out of her mind and switched back and forth between rage and sorrow — one moment screaming accusations, the next asking me to forgive her. While she screamed at me, I passed out, addled by alcohol and sleep-deprived.

I opened my eyes just in time to see the flash of a butcher knife as Charla brought it down in a wide arc. She was half-dressed and wild-eyed. I reached up and gripped her arm to stop the blade, which still went an inch deep into my flesh. I managed to wrest the knife out of her hands and held her until she calmed down. Finally, she relented and began to cry.

"Baby, I'm not mad at you," she said in a warbling voice, as the tears rolled down her cheeks. "I just want you to die and then kill myself so we can be together in heaven."

I felt the familiar blackness closing in tight. I gripped her shoulders and gave her a shake. "Listen to me! There is no heaven. I have no intention of going into a hole in the ground for you or anyone else."

I began cursing God and myself for allowing things to get so messed up. I was a respected electrician. I worked very hard and had always cared for my family. I never failed to pay my bills and to follow through with my obligations to everyone. What was happening to me felt unfair and criminal.

I vowed never to drink again.

Charla's obsession with the idea of our tandem deaths persisted. Periodically, she attempted suicide and also made attempts on my life. She continued to visit institutions and drank almost uncontrollably when she was "off the wagon." At other times, she seemed perfectly lucid.

As hard as I worked, I had trouble keeping up with the bills from Charla's frequent hospitalizations. Meanwhile, I was in a mess of my own. I learned later on that I was living something called a "dry drunk." I left the bottle alone, all right, but the alcohol managed to seep back in just the same and scramble everything up. I was mad with anger.

During one of her sane moments, Charla suggested marriage counseling.

"Don't you think we have enough bills?"

"It's our marriage. Isn't that more important than money?"

"It doesn't matter how important it is! We don't have the money. No, no, no!"

I didn't add that I thought there was absolutely zero chance counseling could help us. Charla had been in and out of psychiatric institutions for years and, rather than improving, had gotten worse and worse.

However, I agreed after Charla found an offer in the paper for free marriage counseling each week at the local library.

We arrived for the first session and sat down as the facilitator passed out brochures and booklets. Then he started reading from the Bible.

I was livid. Ever since my father's death, whenever anyone tried to talk to me about God or the Bible, I exploded in anger. I was on the verge of walking out, but I thought about Charla. My father's voice came back to me: "If you tell someone you will do something, you do it." So I stayed, although I didn't hear another word that was said that night.

Because of my commitment, I continued to attend the

HAND ON MY SHOULDER

weekly sessions without really participating. Then I started listening to the discussions and even doing a bit of reading. Little by little, I was drawn deeper into the group because of my commitment to Charla.

Before long, we were attending church services, then Alcoholics Anonymous meetings as well.

Throughout all of this, I told myself I was doing what was necessary for my family and completely resisted any deference to God or, as the AA people put it, a "higher power." Once, while sitting in an AA meeting, I blew up at one of the regulars I had come to despise because of his habit of challenging everything I said or did. I called him "Mr. Boy" since he was always calling me "Boy." Around the fourth or fifth time he did this, I challenged him to a fight from clear across the room.

Not only did he keep calling me "Boy," he continued challenging me on all kinds of issues, including his favorite — my contention that God was a fairytale. At some point, Mr. Boy made a statement I couldn't dismiss: "It's kind of hard to hate someone you don't believe in." That one remark helped me to take AA's 12 steps to recovery more seriously. I began to work them in earnest and continued going to different churches with Charla.

꾕꾕꾕

I saw a doctor after passing blood for months and was told I had Crohn's disease. It was a serious illness, but my attitude was matter-of-fact. I had endured many things in

New BEGINNINGS

this life. What was one more? Charla, however, was angry because I was so casual about it.

I was driving around one day in June 1992 and stopped by the Muskingum County Fairgrounds, where I enjoyed going for walks. There was a large tent in the middle of the racetrack. I could hear music coming from it.

Music had been a central part of my life for as long as I could remember, though I hadn't had much occasion to enjoy it for a very long time. Now, hearing the music bursting from the tent took me back to childhood, when I had kicked around my family's farm listening to Grandma and Grandpa S play, where my father had taught me how to play guitar. I walked closer.

It was a tent revival. The music continued on as the band went through its repertoire. I could hear the instruments with perfect distinction. The singer's voice was clear and strong. Every word he sang seemed directed at me.

Memories of my childhood came flooding back. I felt the peace and joy that had been my companion as I was growing up, before my parents divorced. I thought of the hours I had spent with Dad strumming guitar and singing together. I remembered vividly the many mornings I spent in church as a child, reciting different scripture verses. I remembered my grandfather, Reverend Norley, and how his huge hands danced in the air as he spoke from the pulpit.

Something inside was pulling me, then pushing me to

HAND ON MY SHOULDER

my knees. I fought hard. I had long told myself that I would kneel for no one. But I wasn't strong enough. As my dark resolve began to weaken, I felt a tremendous surge of peace and comfort flow through me. I sobbed as I prayed in an intensifying deluge of grief. I hadn't cried since my father had died. Now I couldn't stop. I ended up on my knees in the grass, where I began to ask God to forgive me.

Suddenly, I felt a hand on my shoulder. I jumped up and turned quickly. No one was there! I was standing by myself, with the people of the tent revival far off in the field. *What was that?*

For as long as I could remember, I had refused to allow people to put their hands on me. It was a rule. In my mind, physical contact was to be reserved for husbands and wives and very few others. In reality, it was one of the many ways I had shut people out of my life.

I went back to kneeling and cried even harder. Again, I felt the hand — on my back now. This time I didn't move. I kept talking to God and begging him to forgive me. I began to think about all the people I had hurt and the many times I had denied Jesus. For 10 years, I hadn't said his name without a curse word in the sentence. I had been mean and hateful and done physical harm to many men. Not only did I need forgiveness for the many wrongs I had done — I needed to be freed from the crippling rage that consumed me. My whole body went limp and weak as I continued to pray.

Finally, I stood up and lifted my hands as a feeling of

New BEGINNINGS

warmth washed over me. I felt the love of Jesus and finally believed that he accepted me as I was.

After sleeping like a baby all that night, I got up and told my wife everything.

"I've been rescued!" I almost shouted across the dining room table. Charla sat with a puzzled look on her beautiful face, her hand frozen as it clutched a piece of toast.

"It's what I've needed for such a long time! God has taken all my rage and hatred away," I told her.

It would take years, but Jesus took my hard heart and made it soft again. I can laugh, love and feel the hurt and pain of others. He is the best friend I have ever had. I'm not perfect, and I still fail, but I know he'll never leave me alone.

The following week, I was listening to sample CDs at a Christian bookstore and came across a song called "Old Man is Dead" and almost jumped out of my shoes, especially as I listened to the words.

I gave my life to Jesus,
And the old man is dead.

"That is me!" I shouted, then blushed as I looked up and saw the other customers laughing at my reaction.

I started to explain what was going on, but a lady next to me just held up her hand. "God is trying to tell you something. Just listen."

I sang the song to Susie, who led the teaching ministry

HAND ON MY SHOULDER

at the church Charla and I had been attending. It was the beginning of my music ministry.

Charla and I continued bouncing around from church to church, finding a mixed bag of blessings and disappointments in each. Meanwhile, I continued doing my step work in AA.

Times of testing came fast and hard on the heels of my reconciliation with God. Charla stopped attending church with me and resumed drinking heavily. Everything else started up again as well — the unfaithfulness, the trips to the mental hospitals and the violence. God's presence in my life is the only explanation I can think of for how I was able to tolerate what was happening. I told myself again and again that I couldn't possibly change my wife. Instead, I prayed for her fervently and often. I lost count of the times I awoke just in time to prevent her from plunging a knife into me. Each time, God woke me so I could roll out of the way. The love I felt for her exceeded the limits of human endurance. I'm convinced it was because of Jesus, whose own love for this shattered woman flowed through me day after day.

It wasn't long before I visited a church called Trinity Full Gospel after hearing positive comments from some of my friends. Those same friends were there when I walked into the sanctuary. I received hugs of greeting from them and even from some people I had never met. Pastor Terry Rowland, a big man with a fiery preaching style, gave a sermon about listening to God and obeying his instructions. While he preached, I watched his every move

New BEGINNINGS

and questioned what I was feeling. Somehow I felt like God was speaking to me. *This is the place for you.*

~~~

My Crohn's disease worsened steadily as I literally shrank. One day, I stood on the scale looking incredulously at the digital readout: 147. I was a man who had once weighed 220 pounds, a power lifter who could physically do anything I wanted. Now I was unable to make it to the bathroom on my own, soiling myself as I crawled along the floor, often collapsing in exhaustion.

In June 1995, I was given four months to live. After some prayer, I decided to undergo surgery. If I lived, I would have a "J pouch" and an ileostomy bag attached to my body. My thinking was that if the operation failed, I would end up in heaven. It was actually a desirable outcome. My whole family gathered around before I went under anesthesia. Even Charla was there. I sang "Amazing Grace" as they proceeded. My voice became muted as they put the mask over my face.

When I awoke, I saw the smiling faces of Charla, Mandy and my mother. They all interrupted each other trying to tell me how well the surgery had gone. The doctor reported that he had never before had a patient whose vitals didn't "flutter" during surgery of any kind, let alone a surgery as long as the one I had undergone — 17 hours, during which the doctors had tag-teamed through the various steps in the process.

HAND ON MY SHOULDER

I just smiled at my family and said, "Praise God! Piece of cake." Everyone laughed — including me, even though it hurt.

I was given strict instructions to walk daily during my recovery. Charla went on the walks with me. After one such walk, we returned home, where Charla told me to lie down on the couch while she prepared lunch for us — a sandwich for her and baby food for me.

I planned to take a nap and then do some more walking.

I was awakened some time later by a knock on the door. I called for Charla to get it, but she didn't answer me. After several tries, I managed to roll off the couch and get to my feet. As I walked gingerly toward the door, I yelled, "Come in!"

The biggest sheriff I had ever seen walked through the door.

"Are you Mr. Addison?" he asked.

Something was wrong. His hat was in his great big hands. I saw a heaviness in his eyes. I was terrified.

"Yes, I'm Mr. Addison."

The sheriff told me that Charla had driven to a nearby gas station, purchased a six-pack of beer and a small gas can, which she filled with gas. Then she drove out to a back road behind our home, drank the beer, poured the gasoline over her body and lit herself on fire with the cigarette lighter.

"I'm sorry, Mr. Addison. Your wife is dead."

I collapsed on the kitchen floor, crying uncontrollably.

New BEGINNINGS

The sheriff knelt down beside me and talked to me for some time. He kept wanting to help me up off the floor, but I stayed put. Eventually, he left. I remained on the floor for a great while, unable to move. I couldn't escape the thought of my beautiful Charla, overcome with anguish, destroying herself with fire. She had been such a lovely lady, so shapely and pretty. She was always sharply dressed and perfectly groomed. I couldn't imagine how she could burn herself up. I prayed and prayed for God to let it be nothing but a horrible dream. However, it was not.

Sometime later, my sister Adrianne showed up and sat on the floor crying with me for a long time. She stayed with me all that night. In the morning, I made her go home. "You have a family to take care of," I said and sent her out the door. Later on, I received a visit from Pastor Rowland. He visited me often over the next several days. During these visits, I tried to talk but could only cry. Pastor Rowland prayed with me each time he visited, and whenever he did, I felt God's peace settle over me.

Other members of my congregation came as well, every time the doors of the church were open, to drive me to services. I can't imagine how I would have coped without them. I felt a powerful sense of being accepted by the other members. Many people I didn't even know reached out to me even as I lumbered in and out of church wearing baggy shirts and huge sweatpants because of my incisions and the ileostomy bag.

I literally healed there in our sanctuary, absorbing the

HAND ON MY SHOULDER

music and the messages from the pulpit. I especially enjoyed listening to Pastor Rowland pray. There was always such sincerity and passion in his voice. In his life, both personal and professional, there was alignment between his words and his actions. In a very natural way, he became my friend and mentor.

Several weeks after Charla's death, Pastor Rowland sat on my porch talking with me. It was midday.

"Pastor, what would you do if your wife died?" I asked.

His hand swept over his chin. "I don't really know," he said finally. "I'm not faced with that situation. However, I'd like to think I would press in harder to God for his guidance."

I took that answer to heart. Not long afterward, I resumed my music ministry, which later presented an opportunity to play for my church's worship team and also travel around to different churches to play and speak about everything Jesus has done for me.

My doctor also casually started referring to my malady as "inflammatory bowel disease," rather than "Crohn's disease," perhaps as a way of avoiding the unexplainable — *that I had been healed.*

തതത

Two years after losing Charla, I was at a church service and noticed a new family I had never seen before — a beautiful blond woman standing with a man and another woman, both younger.

New BEGINNINGS

I made my way across the sanctuary to greet them. The blond woman introduced herself as Marie. The younger man and woman were her son, Stan, and her daughter, Kristy. I made it a point to talk to them each time I saw them. I had learned that Marie was single and had come out of an abusive marriage. I also couldn't help noticing each time I saw her that Marie had the most beautiful blue eyes.

I got up the nerve to ask her to dinner. She refused. The next week, I asked her again. Again, she refused.

For the next few weeks, I played it cool and just greeted her as she came and went with her family. But finally, I decided to ask her one more time. This time, she accepted. My heart raced. We set a time and a date and then parted.

Marie was very easy to talk to, and I enjoyed every minute we spent together. However, I was cautious and sought the advice of Pastor Rowland.

"I've been watching you," he said before I could even get it all out.

"You have?"

"Yes, I have. I think if you two keep God in your relationship, all will be blessed."

Blessed it was and is. Marie and I were married in November 1997. I went from having no family of my own to having two grown children, who call me Dad, and three small grandchildren.

I am surrounded by family today — and not only because of Marie. My next-door neighbor is my youngest

HAND ON MY SHOULDER

sister, Mandy, now a 43-year-old woman, still as strong and independent as ever.

Over the years, the activities of Trinity Full Gospel have filled more and more of my life. The music outreaches and mission trips have enriched me beyond measure. But the people have made the largest impact on me — especially the ones I have been able to bless.

☙☙☙

Jack and I became friends when I started picking him up for work in the mornings. We lived in the same town and usually drove into outlying towns for work. The trips were often long enough to permit us to speak about all sorts of things. The subject of religion came up frequently. As much as I enjoy telling others what God has done for me, I am always careful to respect a person's wishes. Jack is an agreeable man and readily listened to me as I told pieces of my story to him.

However, Jack had something of an obstacle before him in that he was about as solid a guy as I've ever met. He is a hard worker, honest and trustworthy. He cares faithfully for his family and treats everyone well. No one ever has a bad word to say about him, and I would have been hard put to find any fault in him. Still, he listened to my story and heard the urgency in my voice when I related how much I needed a Savior. I often wondered if he felt his own need for Christ.

I found out one morning as we drove to work

New BEGINNINGS

watching the sun's rays push up over the horizon in an expanding pool of orange. We were quiet for several miles when he asked his question.

"Say, Rick. I've been listening to you talk about Jesus quite a bit. I respect religious people, particularly the ones who put their money where their mouths are. But other than what you said about going to heaven, what's the big deal? What could be so important about embracing this Jesus of yours?"

I paused a moment before I answered. "Jack, we're both family men. If you give any weight to what the Bible says, then I'm going to tell you why. *We are responsible for the salvation of our families.*"

To this day, I don't know where I came up with that statement, but it was exactly what Jack needed to hear. As soon as we pulled into the parking lot, he committed his life to Jesus as we prayed together in my truck.

I am convinced that I serve a God who is an artist and a master archer. His shots never miss. He gave me just the right words for Jack that morning, just as he knew how badly I needed to feel his hand on my shoulder those many years ago. Life has been a wild ride, but I don't regret a second of it. In fact, I can't wait to see what's next.

A MOTHER'S PLEA
The Story of Michelle
Written by Ameerah Collins

Crushed by grief, I crumbled to the nursery's floor and propped my head against the empty crib. Searing hot tears trickled down my face as I gazed at my protruding stomach and clutched at the material covering it. Hopelessness infected my mind like a disease, gnawing at my insides.

I'm empty, unraveled. How can I survive this loss?

I just wished for the prior few days to disappear and never resurface.

I could numb this if I wanted. No more tears. No more pain.

I opened my mouth to release a scream, but a mere whisper of whines filled the air. Images of me in the delivery room bombarded my mind. I could see myself pushing as sweat glistened across my brow and my measured breathing quickened in pace. I saw my devoted husband at my side with my parents and sister-in-law snapping away with her camera as the beautiful sound of my baby's cry echoed throughout the room.

Now I'll never hear his cry again.

The entire scene flooded my memory before a wretched sob finally broke free from my constricted throat. *Was it all my fault?*

New BEGINNINGS

❧❧❧

Throughout my childhood, my parents were always my loyal companions and loudest cheerleaders. My two brothers and I were raised in church and had great morals instilled in us. Like prayer, it was very important to our family. Bowing our heads before dinner, clasping our hands in times of despair or falling to our knees at bedtime was like second nature to us. Such guidance followed into my adulthood, and I attempted to never stray from those teachings.

For me, rebelling from your parents' teachings was unthinkable. I knew all kids weren't fortunate enough to have sober-minded and steady parental figures in their lives, but my parents were great people. They were wise, experienced and wanted the best for me. If I disobeyed their teachings, I knew my life would be a mess. And I wanted an easy life — a life without difficulties and drama. However, it would be a while before I realized that there are some things I simply had no control over and escaping hardships wouldn't be as easy as I thought.

In 1990, I started college. Two years later, I married my high school sweetheart, Derrek. We both dreamed of becoming educators and having a house full of kids. Like me, Derrek grew up in church. It was during this time that we recognized our need to grow up and establish our own personal connection with God.

Soon, I didn't just believe in God, I fell in love with him. I wanted him to approve of my lifestyle. I wanted

A MOTHER'S PLEA

God to know that I was serious about him, and I'd go above and beyond to please him. Derrek and I were so young, just barely hitting our 20s when we decided to give God our all. Our friends partied pretty hard and just couldn't understand why we weren't into the party scene, too. We tried to explain that being surrounded by drugs, dirty dancing, sex and alcohol didn't appeal to us, but it was hard for them to grasp.

"C'mon guys! Stop being a goody-two-shoes!" Several of our friends stood in our doorway holding beers. "Since when is it a crime to drink a little? It's not like you're going to get wasted. We just want to chill."

Derrek spoke up through their snickers. "Look, we're just not into drinking. We've decided to focus on God and his plans for us. We don't want any distractions … getting drunk is a pretty big one."

Derrek and I always refused invitations to events that we knew would be crawling with drunken folks, smoke, violence or filthy conversations. The college parties on our campus could get pretty wild, and we felt certain God didn't want us in that atmosphere. Eventually, our friends distanced themselves from us and no longer invited us to hang out. We felt hurt that they didn't respect our beliefs and even felt ostracized from them, but God had been dealing in our hearts for quite a while, and we believed he understood us. The desire to engage or even entertain those sort of settings disgusted us, and God knew that. When at times we wished to fit in and be "normal" college students, we felt like Jesus covered us in his love, and we

New BEGINNINGS

no longer felt alienated. We may have been loners in our trust, love and loyalty to God, but we felt sure we fit right in with Jesus.

With this in mind, my understanding of God slowly changed. In church, I was always taught that Jesus was the son of God, and he suffered a great death for me, but the knowledge of such a drastic display of love never truly registered. I understood that his death made it possible for me to enter heaven one day. I got that I was God's child, and he loved me. But that love became real when Derrek and I made the decision to really place our marriage and future family in God's hands. We refused to take Jesus' death for granted. If he loved us enough to *die* for us, why not love Jesus enough to *live* for him? No matter what, I was determined to follow God.

Derrek and I began to pray more and read our Bible and, in doing so, found our love for God increased. Learning of Jesus' love for us was amazing, and we knew he was worthy of everything we could give him. Whether it was love, time or trust, it all belonged to God. We also had a yearning to do things right: solidify our marriage, stabilize our careers, then have children. I believed if I lived the way God wanted me to then bad times wouldn't come my way.

After we graduated, Derrek and I obtained great teaching positions in the same school district. A few years later, I gave birth to our first son, Patrick. Though the pregnancy was normal, Patrick had respiratory trouble. Nationwide Children's Hospital worked carefully with

A MOTHER'S PLEA

him. I remember being frustrated because I knew Derrek and I had done everything right according to our church upbringing. I felt slighted by God.

I sat up in my hospital bed with Derrek and my mother at my side. My knee bobbled up and down as I ran a hand through my messy hair.

"I just don't get this," I mumbled with a touch of harshness in my voice. "Why is this happening to us? We're good people. We're *good*, solid people. This shouldn't be —"

"Why not you, Michelle?" Mom's soft yet authoritative voice broke through my wallowing and struck a chord within me. Guilt instantly poured over me as Mom eyed Derrek and me. "Should you be exempt from such pain and struggle just because you love God?"

"No," I barely whispered. "But you and Dad always said we were God's children, and I just thought that meant we were protected from pain."

"Everyone goes through obstacles, Michelle. Even people like you and Derrek."

My mother was right. I believe God spoke through her to me. She'd always had a way of keeping me grounded, often teaching me a lesson when I didn't know there was one to be learned. Through that experience with my first child, I began to realize my love for God didn't exempt me from pain and struggle. Instead, if I let it, God's love for me would help me overcome my obstacles.

Several days later, we brought Patrick home. Though he was hooked up to a heart monitor and breathing

New BEGINNINGS

machine, I was happy he was okay. Patrick wasn't even a year old when I found out I was pregnant again. But just like Patrick, Justin was born with complications.

I delivered Justin six weeks early. His lungs weren't fully developed, and just as he was born, he was swiftly snatched from my arms and transported to Nationwide Children's Hospital for neonatal treatment. I was hopeful for what the doctors could do for him and spent many nights praying for God to look after our baby. After spending two weeks in the hospital developing his lungs and learning to breathe and eat on his own, Justin came home with us.

Finally, the dream of having a house full of children was steadily transpiring. I'd always felt as if my true purpose on earth was to be a mother, to surround myself with children and be a constant caregiver to them. My kids at the school and Patrick and Justin were just a small fraction of what I truly desired.

In 2002, I gave birth to our first daughter, Angel, and a year later I had Aria. Their pregnancies were normal, and I was thankful they didn't have to suffer through any complications.

I suppose some people wondered why I continuously popped out baby after baby. I suspect they talked and gossiped about our suddenly huge family and desire to expand it, but I didn't care. Being a mother simply felt like the most natural thing I'd ever been.

A MOTHER'S PLEA

☙☙☙

A few years later, I was four months pregnant when we decided to take a vacation to Pennsylvania and visit a water park with the kids. My parents were traveling with us, and during a pit stop, I went inside to relieve my bladder.

While using the bathroom, I noticed I was lightly bleeding, but it was more like spotting. I quickly wadded up more tissue and groaned when additional blood appeared. I recalled my obstetrician saying bleeding during a pregnancy was normal. However, I knew I'd never bled with my other babies. As I trudged back to the noisy van, I tried to calm myself and cease the worrying, but I knew something was wrong.

On the first night of our vacation, Derrek and I settled into our hotel room. I used the bathroom before hitting the sack and shuddered at the sight of blood again. What was spotting earlier in the day had steadily become heavier and darker.

I lay down beside Derrek with a heaviness weighing on my heart. Sharp, razor-like pains shot through my abdomen. I tried to ignore it and consider the words of my doctor before falling asleep.

I awoke in the middle of the night feeling weak and feverish. I felt a pool of warm liquid surrounding my bottom and thighs. Fear rumbled in the pit of my gut, then ripped its way up my chest as I pushed the comforter away and whimpered and trembled at what I saw. I covered my

New BEGINNINGS

mouth with my shaky palm. I was lying in a puddle of crimson blood. It seeped into the bed sheets and covered me as if I'd dipped the bottom half of my body in a bucket of blood.

I hastily gripped Derrek's arm and shook him. "Derrek, wake up! I'm bleeding! I think something's wrong with the baby!" I tried to keep my yelps and crying to a minimum, not wanting to wake the children, but I was so scared and frantic.

"Oh, my God." Derrek's eyes widened at the amount of blood. I looked at him, and my lips quivered as the notion of losing our baby raced through my mind.

"Hey, look at me. It'll be okay." He kissed my forehead before flying from the bloody mattress and racing out of the room.

Seconds later my parents rushed in behind Derrek. Mom phoned our pastor. Though it was in the wee hours of the night, he was there for our call. Pastor Rowland immediately began to pray. "God, we ask for complete healing right now. We know that you are more than capable of fixing whatever issue is going on within Michelle. Please heal her and the baby. Amen."

Derrek rushed me to the local hospital. Upon entering the emergency room, the odor of bleached sheets, bitter medications and disinfectant attacked my nostrils. The atmosphere was cold, and the people didn't seem as caring as they might have been toward my delicate situation. The nurses pulled us into a room and readied me for a pelvic exam and an ultrasound. I watched as they bustled

A MOTHER'S PLEA

around, not speaking to me much, before a doctor entered.

For a minute, I didn't know what was happening. But when the doctor lowered his voice and sorrow tugged at his lips, I knew I'd lost my baby. I couldn't stop shaking and crying, even though Derrek had me pressed into his side. I slumped over the hospital bed and shook my head in dismay as heartbroken sobs, cries that sounded nothing like me, left my mouth.

"I'm sorry," the doctor said, "but I believe you lost the baby the last time you urinated. The spotting and bleeding you were concerned about … those were the symptoms of this miscarriage. I am terribly sorry for your loss."

"No, no, no." I cried into Derrek's shoulder and looked up at the doctor. "This can't be right. How could this happen? I didn't do anything wrong!"

"Of course not," the doctor said, nodding. "Sometimes these things happen. Nevertheless, we'll need to perform a D&C as soon as possible."

Voicing such a common procedure for women who suffered from miscarriages triggered more sobs. I was horrified that I'd lost my precious baby in the hotel bathroom. The tears and the harsh bellows coming from the hollows of my stomach wouldn't cease. That baby belonged to us, and yet we would never get to kiss and hold our little one. It was all so surreal. Feelings of loss and total emptiness, emotions I'd never encountered before, consumed me.

The following day, the surgeons readied me for the

New BEGINNINGS

dilation and curettage procedure. The nurses laid me on a gurney and placed my legs in stirrups. I wanted to run and hide from the pain of my loss, but I couldn't move as the procedure began.

❧❧❧

In 2007, Derrek and I visited our children's pediatrician to discuss having more children. Though my boys had difficulties right after childbirth, our doctor didn't believe my miscarriage would negatively affect any future pregnancies.

Derrek and I later visited my obstetrician, Dr. Tillman. She was very close to the family and had been with me through the births of all my children. As she entered her office, Derrek and I sat beside one another and awaited her advice.

"Michelle, Derrek," Dr. Tillman said with a soft smile, "I really don't foresee any complications in regard to you two having more children. The unfortunate miscarriage shouldn't have any adverse effect on future pregnancies."

I turned toward Derrek and grinned. "We haven't had a baby in the house in so long. I miss being the mother of a newborn baby. If it's safe …" I looked over at Dr. Tillman again. She fervently nodded when I sought her reassurance. "All right, let's do it."

Months later I found out I was pregnant. Derrek and I constantly prayed and asked God to give us a baby. For years we'd had his named picked out, and I couldn't wait

A MOTHER'S PLEA

for Elijah to enter our world. The pregnancy was normal, except for a little fluid built up in my womb. One day, Dr. Tillman called me and inquired about coming in for an ultrasound. She was concerned about the fluid, but I didn't see any need to worry. Dr. Tillman had been with me through five pregnancies, and I trusted her.

"We need to induce labor," Dr. Tillman said as she wiped the cold, sticky gel from my large belly. "It's nothing to worry about," she quickly said when my eyebrows arched. "I just don't like the buildup of fluid. I think it's best if we get this little guy out here with us."

The afternoon of February 12, 2008, my labor was induced. It was slow due to all the excess water and took longer than expected.

My parents, Derrek and my sister-in-law, Janet, crowded into the delivery room and cheered me on as I pushed little Elijah into our world. I could feel the burn of sweat falling into my eyes as Derrek matched my measured breathing as if he was pushing, too. I gripped his hand as Janet happily snapped pictures, waiting for Elijah.

His high-pitched cry brought tears to my eyes as he was cleaned, wrapped in a blanket and finally brought to my arms. I couldn't wait to hold him. He was 8 pounds, 3 ounces and 21 inches long. I cooed at him and grinned at my elated husband as Elijah opened his bright blue eyes, and I stroked his fuzzy blond hair. He was the spitting image of his father and brothers.

Initially, there didn't seem to be anything seriously wrong with him, but his body temperature was a little off.

New BEGINNINGS

The nurses transported him to a warmer intensive care unit room for his temperature to regulate. I didn't feel the need to worry. I knew I'd prayed to God for a healthy baby, and I believed he'd given us just that. I believed that he'd easily be fixed up, and after that, we would put him in his car seat and take him home to meet his sisters and brothers. I assumed he would be fine. I was wrong, though. Elijah was anything but fine.

Over the next day, I became anxious. I didn't get to hold Elijah often. The doctors didn't want Derrek or me to fuss with him because he wasn't eating like he was supposed to. They said if I didn't bother him much he'd get healthy sooner. I rarely touched him, held him or even saw his eyes because he slept so much. All I could really do was sing "Jesus Loves Me" to him and watch him blink his eyes at the sound of my voice.

After spending two days in the hospital, I was released. However, I had no plans of going home without Elijah. The hospital allowed me to stay on another floor. Elijah began having problems with the oxygen level in his body, and his temperature still wasn't regulating.

As I sat beside his small bed, the doctors informed me he wasn't gaining much weight. I sighed at my little one in his hospital onesie. The beeping of the machines, the tubes connected to his body and the nurses' constant need for blood drawn was draining me. My comfort level was low, and there was a sinking sensation in my gut.

"Excuse me, dear." A woman with silvery-white hair and a kind smile leaned against the doorframe. She had

A MOTHER'S PLEA

two long knitting needles in one hand, a blue knitted cap in the other. "I heard your baby wasn't doing well, and I know you must get tired of seeing him in that hospital getup."

"My husband and I bought him so many clothes," I said, softly chuckling. "He can't wear them, though. They'll get in the way of drawing blood and … stuff. I'm just praying he'll get well. I want to take him home so badly."

"Aw, yes." The woman nodded and wobbled next to me in her flimsy gown and powder-blue slippers. "You can't get any rest in a hospital. If they're not drawing blood, they're taking your vitals. If they're not taking your vitals, they're hooking you up to some machine. But I made your boy something. I figured you'd want to see him in something a bit more normal."

She offered the blue knitted cap to me, and I gripped the soft material in my fingers. It was plush and small, just like Elijah. I softly tugged it on Elijah's head and stroked his cheek. "Thank you. It really means a lot."

Soon after, my parents and Derrek's parents came to visit, and they all beamed at Elijah's blue cap. They brought my children with them, and they were all able to kiss and hug Elijah. As I observed my children showing their new little brother such love and affection, I was hopeful that Elijah would get well and all would be right with our world. I just knew his pain would settle, his eating and breathing complications would go away and there would be no restrictions on how much I held him.

New BEGINNINGS

The day after Valentine's Day, Elijah took a turn for the worse. The doctors noticed his weight gain was not picking up. They performed an ultrasound to figure out the primary issue to his failing health. They discovered holes in his lower intestines and a bowel infection. The tones of the doctors were normal, and they expressed no urgency. All we had to do was transport him to Nationwide Children's Hospital where he could receive the utmost care.

My heart still overflowed with hope as Derrek and I sped down the freeway, following behind the ambulance that carried our son. During this time, I didn't feel the need to worry. Words of prayer continuously flowed through my mind and dripped from my tongue as I pulled into the parking garage.

I burst through the wide doors of the emergency room and skidded to a halt before the front desk. Derrek sprinted in after me; his hands gripped the edge of the counter causing his knuckles to turn white. I dropped my head against the counter when the nurse informed me the staff was already readying Elijah for surgery. Though I knew all would be right, I wanted to look at him. I wanted to see his beautiful blue eyes and tell him Jesus loved him. I needed to touch his pudgy little fingers to not just reassure him, but to reassure myself as well.

"What are they doing to him? What is going on?" I questioned as I rubbed at my weary eyes. I sighed as the nurse beckoned someone else over and exchanged a few words with him. I realized the man was a doctor.

A MOTHER'S PLEA

"Can you please tell us how our son is?" Derrek's voice hitched in concern. "Will he be all right?"

"Yes," the doctor said, nodding, "he is getting prepped for surgery as we speak. The surgeon will reconstruct his intestines. Essentially, he will cut out the parts of your son's intestines with the holes in it. It's a procedure that we perform often, and I don't believe you have anything to worry about."

I was relieved at the doctor's explanation, but I was still bombarded with worrisome thoughts. The burning of tears building up in my eyes finally spilled over, and Derrek whispered loving words of encouragement in my ear as he led me over to a chair in the waiting room. We prayed together and asked God to be in the operating room with our little one.

After the surgery, the surgeon entered the waiting room and led Derrek and me to a more private area. He shut the door and welcomed us to sit down.

"I'm very optimistic about the success of this surgery," he said. "I don't foresee any other serious health issues in Elijah's near future. He will definitely need a few more surgeries over the years and as he grows older, but nothing life-threatening."

"Oh, thank God." Derrek released a shuddering sigh. He peered at me with a wide grin, and I returned it with joyful tears in my eyes. Derrek cupped my cheeks in his hands as he pressed his forehead against mine. "You hear that? He's going to be okay. Elijah will be okay."

But would he really be okay? I thanked God for saving

New BEGINNINGS

my baby, but I couldn't help but wonder about Elijah's future. I worried about his life as he grew older. Would he be able to play with other children? Would his food choices be limited? How would his surgeries play into our busy lives? Was I ready for a child with health needs?

Guilt soon washed over me. How could I think such selfish thoughts? How could I, an educator and lover of all children, second guess a child with delicate health needs? I clenched my hands at my sides and silently berated myself for despicable thoughts that were so unlike me.

We followed the surgeon down the hall into Elijah's room, and I couldn't wait to see him. As we entered, I gasped at the sight of him. Monitors, wires, a breathing apparatus and tubes flowed from his tiny form, but he still looked good. *What was I thinking second guessing my sweet little fighter?* Derrek and I touched him, kissed him and talked to him. We still weren't allowed to hold him, but knowing we could fill his room with stuffed animals and surround his bed with pictures of his siblings made us feel better.

We eventually called our parents and informed them of everything that was happening. Pastor Rowland was contacted, as well as various members of our church, Trinity Full Gospel. Though Pastor Rowland was on a mission trip, his children came and visited us in the hospital. It was such a comfort knowing not only were family and friends behind Derrek and me, but our church family was, too. It was amazing how devoted a congregation could be to one family.

A MOTHER'S PLEA

On February 16, just a day after Elijah's surgery, Derrek's parents brought all the kids to visit. I missed them so much that I played with them like a child in the recreation room. They wanted to see Elijah — practically begged to. But I didn't want the tubes and machines to scare them, so I decided it was best not to implant such a traumatic image in their minds.

As I sat looking at my children play and Derrek talk to our parents, a sense of urgency suddenly overwhelmed me. It was like something was pushing me to return to Elijah. I believed it was God telling me that Elijah needed me. I immediately cut the visit short. Derrek's parents took the kids home, and my parents stayed at the hospital with us.

When I entered Elijah's room, I knew everything was plummeting. Several nurses surrounded him and worked diligently to stabilize him. They were panicking and raising their voices at one another. One sprinted out of the room to fetch a doctor. I could barely move my legs as Derrek hounded the nurses on what was happening to our son. I wept as I noticed the discoloring of his skin. His lips and fingertips were turning light blue, and his once-creamy skin looked gray. I could see moisture forming on his pale face and his chest moving unevenly.

"What's wrong with my baby?" I cried as I rushed over to his bedside, but a nurse gently pushed me away. I yanked my arm away and screamed for answers. I could feel my mother tugging on me and Derrek's arm wrapped securely around my waist. I didn't realize they were

New BEGINNINGS

holding me up until I sank to the cold floor. "No! What's wrong with my baby?"

"Ma'am." A plump little nurse gripped my shoulders and helped to pull me up. "We're doing everything we can to save him. His body is shutting down, and he's going into shock. We're trying to do all we can to stabilize him. I need you to step back and let us work."

I gave in to her soft demand and bawled my eyes out. I held onto Derrek, as more nurses and doctors plowed into the room. They fiddled with machines, hooked him up to more tubes and poked at his veins. As their shouts and voices grew louder, I realized I needed to plead with God and beg him to save my baby. I had been praying and thanking God ever since Elijah's birth, but I knew I needed to do more. I cried out to Jesus and asked him to intercede for me. I didn't care who witnessed my pleas, I needed God to save my boy, and I wouldn't rest my voice until he did.

As my crying grew worse, I realized I couldn't take seeing my little one in such pain. I couldn't bear to see his face turning a color so stony that it seemed as if death hovered over him. I stumbled out of the room, but my knees buckled, and I almost hit the floor before Derrek caught me. I leaned on his chest and clutched at his shirt, using the material as a tissue to wipe my tears away. The soles of my shoes never hit the floor as he practically dragged and carried me down the hall to an empty room. I heard my mother and father follow us, but I couldn't look at them as a doctor suddenly appeared before us.

A MOTHER'S PLEA

"Elijah's blood isn't flowing to the rest of his body." His voice was low and sorrowful as he licked his lips. "We can perform a surgery that will bypass his heart and pump the blood through his body ... but the success rate is very low. It will be hard on him. He's very fragile right now, but it's completely up to you two what we do next."

In that moment I realized I might not ever take Elijah home. I knew my son was dying, and there was nothing I could do about it. His body was in such distress. I didn't want him to suffer anymore. I peered at Derrek and then my parents as the doctor awaited an answer.

"Give it up to God, Michelle," Mom tenderly whispered, and that was all I needed.

I dropped to my knees. We prayed in the small room and cried out to God. I begged him to heal my baby. I needed God to hear my cry and not take my son away so soon. After about 15 minutes of us constantly praying, my mother touched my shoulder. She had tears in her eyes.

"It's enough," Mom said simply.

Before I could respond, the stout little nurse from earlier opened the door to our private room and said, "Elijah has passed away. I'm so sorry. There was nothing we could do."

We walked back to Elijah's room. My body was so heavy. It felt as if I was lugging a backpack of bricks on my shoulders. As we entered the room and I peered down at his lifeless body, I knew my Elijah was no longer there. The nurses asked me if I wanted to hold him one last time, but I shook my head.

New BEGINNINGS

"You need to hold him," Mom said.

I sat down in the rocking chair near his bed, and the nurse placed him in my arms. I wept. His body was so cold and clammy. My little Elijah was gone. His tiny hand was heavier than before. It wasn't light, soft and warm like I'd remembered. I cried harder, wishing I'd let my other children hold him when they'd come to visit him. If I'd known he would leave so soon, I would have hugged him more and disregarded the doctor's orders of not fussing with him too much.

"I can't. I don't want to hold him anymore," I choked out between heavy sobs and haggard breaths. "Take him. Please, just take him. I can't hold him anymore."

❧❧❧

February 17, 2008 was the worst day of my life. At about 1:30 a.m., Elijah left too soon, and I didn't know what to do with myself. The heavy loss I felt inside was enough to split me to shreds. I kept waiting for someone to wake me. I couldn't believe such a horrifying nightmare was my reality.

My children understood Elijah was in heaven, but that truth didn't alleviate the pain. I watched them weep over their lost brother, and there was nothing Derrek or I could do to make them feel better. Our hugs and shared tears weren't enough. Nothing could bring Elijah back. My kids deemed heaven such a faraway place. They knew they would see Elijah again, but the wait would be hard.

A MOTHER'S PLEA

As I walked into his vacant nursery, I dropped to the floor and leaned against his crib. I stroked the plush carpet with my hands as diapers, baby wipes, lotions and toys suddenly assailed me with their useless presence. I felt like my purpose had been stripped away — like motherhood was something I could no longer truly fulfill. I knew I would always be a mom to my other children, but what kind of mother lost a child? How could being a mother be my purpose in the world if I couldn't protect my kids and keep them from harm — from *death*?

This pain was nothing like the pain I felt during my miscarriage. I hadn't held my little one then, I hadn't seen him with my eyes, and my children weren't old enough to understand why the baby in their mommy's tummy was no longer coming. This ache was unbearable. I wanted it gone. Everyone was going on with his or her life as if I hadn't just lost a gigantic piece of mine, and I hated their happiness. I knew doctors could easily numb my pain with prescribed medication, but I believed God would be upset if I became dependent on drugs instead of him.

Sitting in Elijah's nursery, I began to blame myself for his death. I pushed too hard, I pushed too soon and I shouldn't have induced labor. I kept telling myself it was my fault. My baby was gone because of me. Cruel thoughts struck me so ruthlessly that I burst into tears and accepted what I thought was the pungent truth: Elijah was gone because of me.

When it was time to plan the funeral, I didn't want any part of it. I didn't care about the attire, the casket or the music to be played. Derrek and a close friend handled all the particulars, while I sat there in my own little world. The days crawled, and the nights were nothing but a blur. I didn't necessarily want to die and be with Elijah, but I wanted to just go away. Earth and its complexities and miseries were too much for me.

The funeral was held at our church home, Trinity Full Gospel, and it snowed that morning. Though I didn't realize it at the time, I believe God used the beautiful white snow as a symbol of Elijah's purity and delicateness. Whenever it snows, we remember him. My two brothers and two sons carried Elijah's coffin. More than 250 people filled the church and came to honor his life. I was so overwhelmed with the love and support from our congregation and community. I hadn't known so many people could be impacted by a 5-day-old boy. And though I couldn't speak, my husband and Pastor Rowland said more than I ever could.

"Do not feel sorry for us," Derrek said before the congregation. "But remember the lessons Elijah taught us. Remember how in five days, this little boy changed us so much. He taught us humility, compassion and, most importantly, he brought us closer to God and his son, Jesus. Though we will miss him greatly, we know he's resting in heaven with our Lord."

I bowed my head in an attempt to muffle my cries as Derrek walked back to his seat. I felt him sit next to me and wrap his arm around me, tugging me close. It was something he'd been doing throughout our entire

A MOTHER'S PLEA

situation with Elijah, and I didn't take it for granted. When Pastor Rowland stood up to speak, I couldn't help but tear up even more.

"Oftentimes, we take upon the assumption that everything is going to be all right," Pastor Rowland said. "We think we're going to be able to hold our children a million times throughout their lives, and nothing will take them away from us. But, Derrek and Michelle, I want you to know that you're not alone, and God never left you. He heard your pleas, and he answers all prayers — sometimes it's just not the answer we hope for. We aren't aware of his plans. We don't know what he has in mind. We just have to trust him." Pastor Rowland looked down on me from the pulpit and softly smiled. "And when you get to heaven, Michelle, expect Elijah to give you the grand tour."

As we walked toward the cemetery, there was snow on the ground. The wind blew and gradually dried our tears as wind chimes sounded in the distance. Delicate flowers were piled on top of Elijah's small casket. I looked at my children as we all formed a half circle around the grave. Patrick and Justin were so strong. They didn't shed a tear. Aria, my littlest one, didn't fully comprehend what was occurring, but Angel grasped onto my leg and cried into my dress. She knew exactly what was happening. Her baby brother was gone.

※※※

New BEGINNINGS

For months I went through various stages of grief. I continued to blame myself, the doctors who performed surgery on him and the nurses who couldn't save him. I even went so far as to blame God. I had so much hope in him, and I knew he was capable of healing my son, but he didn't. My mind didn't want to direct such anger toward God, but my heart did. I couldn't fathom why Elijah wasn't good enough to live. Was I that horrible of a mother?

We received more than 200 letters from family and friends. Though I appreciated the love and support, it was bittersweet because it served as a constant reminder of our loss. Holidays meant nothing to me, birthday celebrations were a thing of the past and the days were no longer worth rising for. I had reoccurring dreams of Elijah crying out for me and me being unable to find him. Those dreams did nothing but amplify my feelings of loss and despair. It increased my belief that my purpose had been snatched away right along with Elijah.

Most times I wanted to be left alone. Questions regarding my motherhood kept rising, and I wanted it all to go away. Derrek and my mom stuck close to me and accompanied me to doctor visits. I knew I would refuse any medicine to numb the pain, but they still wanted to keep a close eye on me and ensure I didn't do anything rash.

When our doctors called to discuss the cause of Elijah's death, I thought I was finally going to get an answer, but I was wrong. They were unsure what went

A MOTHER'S PLEA

wrong and why such a sequence of horrific events occurred. They simply said he had a sepsis infection — a condition in which the body fights a severe infection that has infiltrated the bloodstream.

I didn't know what to think. I felt like the doctors were just throwing something out there to make us feel better about his death, but it did the exact opposite. No closure, no ending, no nothing. Even my obstetrician didn't understand what went wrong. She said I was healthy, and nothing should have harmed our baby. I walked out of that doctor's office feeling defeated and confused.

Though it took a while, I accepted my son was simply meant to live in heaven and not on earth. I stopped blaming God and asked for his forgiveness. I began to pray more and discuss my feelings with him. No doctor could ease my pain. Derrek could wipe away my tears, but he could do nothing about the wailing of my heart. Only God could heal me, and when I accepted that, he steadily closed the hole in my heart and filled it with his love.

Though I missed the smell of Elijah's skin, the brightness of his blue eyes and the soft touch of his little fingers, I knew he was safe and free from suffering. Though I longed for him to sit on my lap, look into my eyes and call me mommy, I reassured myself that he was very much loved in heaven. I reminded myself of how good it felt to hold him in my arms, and I constantly looked at all the pictures my sister-in-law snapped of him. I was so thankful that Janet had taken those pictures.

"I want to start praying for more children. I think

New BEGINNINGS

we're ready," Derrek said to me one night. "In no way can we replace Elijah, but I know you, Michelle. You want more children, and I want what you want."

I sat up in bed and looked at him. "People will ridicule us. They'll talk."

"Let them talk," Derrek said, and I nodded. "It doesn't matter what people say, it only matters what God says."

"Our church family won't judge us," I said. "Pastor Rowland and his family won't, either. They'll understand we're not trying to replace Elijah. We just love children."

Derrek said, "I know. And this happened to us for a reason. We've never been closer to God before in our lives. Elijah taught us to cling to Jesus, to pray more and never question God's plan. He will always be our son, but we must push forward, too."

"When we were losing Elijah and we cried out to God, that cry came from deep within. I've never cried out to God like that before. And now," I softly smiled as tears slid down my cheeks, "God has given me such peace with what happened and hope for our future. I want to pray for more children, too. I want to make sure it's what God wants."

That night, Derrek and I began to ask God for more children. We prayed for healthy babies and asked God to continue to strengthen our belief in him. Our church family continued to pray with us, and their prayers helped us along the way. I met other women who experienced the same sort of loss, and we bonded over such difficult times. And just as I'd admired my mother's closeness with God, I steadily developed my own closeness with him.

A MOTHER'S PLEA

In April 2009, I gave birth to my little girl Lillian. In May of 2010, I gave birth to my son Zachery. I was nervous about being judged, but everyone at Trinity Full Gospel calmed my fears. They loved us and prayed for our wellbeing. Though God lessened our grief over Elijah, there were and still are moments when Derrek and I long for him. There are times when I hold his blue knitted cap close to my heart and wonder how his voice would have sounded by now. I think about the joyful and goofy personalities of my boys and Derrek and wonder if he would have been like them. But I thank God for his perfect love and understanding. Though I may have lost my child on earth, I do believe God has made it possible for me to see Elijah again one day in heaven.

In my low moments, I latch onto what Pastor Rowland said at Elijah's funeral. When I get to heaven, I do expect Elijah to give me the grand tour.

HOME SWEET HOME
The Story of Jamie
Written by Karen Heeringa

My sister, my cousin and I walked slowly ahead of my mom and my stepfather, Eric. They took their time, arguing in the parking lot of the mall. This wasn't new to us anymore, but it was still pretty embarrassing. We had been through it many times before.

We jumped into the backseat of our car and waited. My mom and Eric stopped at the back of the car by the trunk and continued to argue. I watched out the rear window of the car and observed their body language. Eric's hands flailed around in the air, Mom's hands at her hips.

I turned to face the front of the car; I wondered if this fight was about my sister and me again.

Abruptly, a heart-stopping crash broke the silence in the backseat. We twisted our heads back and felt the breeze from the cool fall air outside. The back window had shattered. Shards of glass littered the rear dash just behind us; others sprinkled onto our seats and shoulders. In the center of the glassy disaster were Eric's keys.

My mother looked completely humiliated as she glared at the broken window.

No one said anything. Mom and Eric got into the car. He grabbed his keys, started the engine and drove us home with the chilly wind from the exposed back window

New BEGINNINGS

whirling our hair through the air. Mom's sobs broke the awkward silence. We brushed pieces of glass off our seats, stunned nobody was bleeding. The fear I felt then was something that stayed with me for a long time.

❧❧❧

"What is happening? This can't really be happening to us!" I cried as I followed my mom out the front door. I hugged her just before she opened the door and got into her car. I stood in the driveway with my sister and my dad, tears falling down my cheeks. I hugged my arms together, instinctively trying to keep myself warm from the chill in the air, but inside, I felt broken. As my mom's car pulled out of the driveway onto the road, I watched as she wiped her wet cheeks with her hand. I cried as the glow of the taillights grew smaller and smaller in the foggy evening light.

My knees felt weak as I walked back into the house with my dad and sister, who were both crying quietly.

It's difficult to know who you are or who you want to become once your life rips into two different worlds. I was 9 years old, and I would never grow out of the phase of needing my mom. My mom loved me so much, and she was still in my life, but nothing was the same. I missed the little things — her making breakfast for us, laughing and dancing with us in the kitchen and tucking us in at night.

Since I was older than my sister, Jenny, I felt that I needed to take on the role of mothering her. Soon enough,

HOME SWEET HOME

I woke up early and helped Jenny get ready for school. This didn't always go over well. Many times Jenny would declare a rebellion against her older sister.

"You need to brush your hair, Jenny," I would say.

"You can't tell me what to do!" Jenny screamed back. "You're not Mom!"

How could I respond? Of course I wasn't Mom. I didn't want to take on that role. Something clicked in my mind, though, when my parents divorced. I felt like I needed to step up and help out when Dad wasn't home. It just became a part of who I was.

When I woke up and readied my sister for school each morning, my dad snored on the couch.

"Dad, I need you to sign this permission slip." I'd shake his shoulder to try and wake him.

"Okay, Dad, this isn't helping. You need to get up!" I announced.

With a sleepy demeanor, he slowly rose from the couch and signed the paper. Dad worked until midnight and never seemed to make it all the way to his bed.

"And don't forget that Mom's picking Jenny and me up tonight for the weekend," I'd remind him. He nodded his head, yawned and went back to sleep.

Dad never abandoned his responsibilities, but when he was at work, I did my best to clean the house, do the laundry and give Jenny, who was 6 when they got divorced, baths. I would make lunches for both of us for school. I worried about everything. *What if we forget picture day on Wednesday? What if we forget to ask Dad*

New BEGINNINGS

to put money in our field trip envelopes? Why can't things go back to how they were before?

I thought about the vacations we used to take as a family. I thought about carefree days when Mom and Dad would take us to the airport and let us watch the planes take off and land, and take off and land. Life was relaxed. Now I felt surrounded by a cloud of stress. Goodbye carefree childhood, welcome adult worries.

❧❧❧

"Girls, this is your bedroom!" my mother exclaimed as she gave us a tour of her new apartment. She now lived 30 miles away from us, and the decision was made that every weekend we would stay with her.

"Also, I'm thinking about visiting you two next week — maybe we can get some dinner, say, Tuesday night?"

The routines changed. So did our relationships.

Mom and Dad started dating other people. This was an entirely new emotional obstacle for Jenny and me.

Once, we were at a family get-together at our uncle's house on my mom's side of the family. My mom was sitting by her new boyfriend. As my cousins, Jenny and I practiced a dance routine, he leaned over and kissed my mom on the lips. Something inside me grew hot and angry, like the Hulk. I did not like what I saw.

"Mom! We're trying to do this dance, and you're not watching us!" It angered me that she was kissing someone who wasn't my dad, even if Mom and Dad were divorced.

HOME SWEET HOME

I felt nauseous looking at them having a tender moment. *That is not supposed to happen! She's supposed to only kiss Dad,* I thought. *She can't be with this man.*

As our transition period continued on, just like our lives somehow, it was understood that our mom missed us and wanted to be near us as often as possible. We lived with our dad because our parents decided that it would be easier for us to continue to live in the area where we already had friends and a good school to attend. What they didn't seem to realize was that the time I should have been playing with the friends they wanted me to stay in contact with, I now used to keep the house from going into disarray while Dad was working. If I wasn't making dinner, doing the dishes, vacuuming, getting my sister ready for bed or helping her with her homework, I was trying to keep up on my own homework and wellbeing. I felt completely alone.

Sometimes, I would hang out with friends who were considerably older than me because I wanted to escape the reality of my broken family. Spending time with them didn't ease the sadness, especially observing their families, which to me seemed perfect and "whole." I knew my life would never be how theirs looked, and I started to believe I didn't fit in anywhere.

By the time I was 13, it no longer felt like there was a death in the family, but the sorrow and empty feeling still lingered. My dad announced to us that we were going to move to a town called Zanesville. He had worked there for some time now, and he grew annoyed with the one-hour

New BEGINNINGS

trek he made each day and decided we should move there. *Great. More change,* I thought to myself.

Mom would often try to reconcile with my dad when she came to visit her daughters, which ended up being less often now since we lived farther away.

"We should have tried harder — the sort of things you want in the past are so different from what you want now," she would vaguely confess to Jenny and me, never telling us why they had divorced in the first place. All the feelings I felt when they first separated bubbled up, and it felt like I was 9 years old again. I wanted to fix my family's problems, but I just couldn't.

What my mom didn't know, though, was that my dad had found a new girlfriend.

One day I was in the kitchen when I heard voices outside the house. I hopped down the stairs onto the landing to peek out the front door and saw my dad talking to someone. It was a woman.

Jenny noticed, too, and joined me at the door.

"Girls? Hey, girls, come here," my father said, noticing our curiosity with this mysterious woman. It was night time, so I couldn't get a good view of her face until I was right in front of her.

"Nice to meet you," she said to me sweetly.

"You, too," I replied.

"Girls, this is Elise," Dad informed us.

As our conversations continued, Elise seemed to be very outgoing and happy. We didn't know that this was our dad's girlfriend at the time, we just thought she was

HOME SWEET HOME

one of dad's co-workers stopping by to say hello before going home herself.

Not long after our meeting with Elise, we found out that Dad was dating her.

"What's she like?" my mom asked as soon as we told her the news. "Does she stay at the house a lot?"

When Mom picked us up for our occasional dinner together, she seemed very interested in knowing how serious Dad's relationship was. Jenny and I felt caught in the middle. Dad didn't talk about her much around us to make it easier on us, but that soon came to an end.

"Girls, Elise and her two daughters are going to move in with us," he informed us a year after they started dating. "You're going to be sharing a room from now on, and Elise's daughters will be sharing a room, too."

At first, it seemed like a great idea. *Maybe we'll be just like* The Brady Bunch, I thought. Jenny and I were excited to see Dad so happy.

Dad married Elise not long after she and her daughters moved in. Before long, I was walking on eggshells around her. She could be critical, and I felt like I could never meet her standards.

Some of it stemmed from issues with my mother. She knew that my mom tried to reconcile with Dad, and understandably, there was anxiety in knowing that Mom would always be someone who was once married to her husband. It seemed Elise wanted us to think of her as our mom, and she was hurt that we didn't feel that way toward her.

New BEGINNINGS

Dad's attention and affection seemed to drift further from Jenny and me. He seemed focused on Elise and her girls. *Does he care more about their happiness than ours?*

During the week, Jenny and I dealt with the tension at Dad's house. On Fridays, Mom would come and pick us up to take us away for the weekend.

Unfortunately, life at my mom's house soon turned unpleasant and complicated, too.

Mom married Eric, who had a very sensitive temper. He easily became angry over what seemed to me like little things.

"The girls are always leaving the lights on!" Eric would stomp through the house, flip the light switches off and slam the doors shut.

He reminded me of a firecracker, always waiting to go off with the slightest amount of heat. I never felt like I could speak candidly, especially in public, for fear that Eric would get angry and embarrass me in front of people, who would stop and stare.

Going out to dinner was always a test of his patience. "Of course, the waitress got my order all wrong again," he'd say as he rolled his eyes. He would complain long enough to make the server upset and offer him a free meal. I would slouch in my seat, embarrassed, hiding my face from others in the restaurant.

Jenny, my cousin and I went to the mall with my mom and Eric one day to meet Eric's parents for dinner. Afterward, as we were walking around in one of the shops, Mom and Eric began to argue. I don't know what the

HOME SWEET HOME

conversation was about, but I know that it made Eric very upset.

Dad felt that since he was keeping us during the week, Mom should be responsible for buying us school clothes and giving us money for field trips. Mom wondered why that responsibility should fall solely on her. The battles went on. Eric was always touchy about the subject, and he would often get angry. I wondered if this was one of those times.

We decided to leave. As we walked through the parking lot back to the car, my mom and Eric continued to argue. We climbed into the backseat, while they stood outside yelling at each other. Before I knew what was happening, the back window shattered into a burst of crystal pieces. Eric, it seemed, had thrown his keys directly at us. Eric had never physically abused us, but when I saw the glass and the look on his face, I felt fear all the way to my toes. *How much longer until he really hurts us?*

Back at my dad's house, my life was in shambles. Elise wasn't much of a housekeeper, so the chores seemed to fall to Jenny and me. I was working so hard all the time, keeping up with the housework, balancing school and often babysitting my younger stepsisters. I never relaxed. Elise had also made a habit of talking bad about us and our dad in front of other people. I thought Eric's level of negativity was high, but Elise matched him with her constant manipulation. I was miserable.

I wanted to be perfect. But no matter what I did, I always felt like I was upsetting someone or hurting his or

New BEGINNINGS

her feelings. I tried to make everyone happy, but the peace I wanted for my family seemed far out of reach.

In the midst of the drama, I was thankful for the one person in my life who was always there — my sister. Jenny and I argued like sisters often do, but I loved her so much, and I was thankful we had each other for support.

At Trinity Full Gospel, the church I attended with my dad and Elise, there was a youth pastor who would often ask me about my week.

"I haven't seen you at youth group. I hope maybe I'll see you this week!" he told me.

Although going to youth group meant hanging out with other teenagers my age, I still felt shy and uncomfortable.

My youth group traveled to a larger gathering of youth groups in an auditorium one day, and up on the screen, they showed a presentation someone made about going to foreign countries and doing good things in their community.

During a slideshow of different places to go around the world, I saw a photo of some people in Panama, and my heart raced out of my chest. *I have to go there,* I thought.

A man stood up after the presentation and spoke for a brief moment.

"If any of you are interested in going to any of these places I've shown in the presentation, there is going to be a meeting in conference room C right now. This is an opportunity of a lifetime, and I hope to see you all there."

The people started leaving the auditorium, making

HOME SWEET HOME

their way to the groups they came with. A few headed down the hall to go to the mission trip meeting.

"Okay, everyone, let's stick together!" my youth pastor said. "Let's all make our way to the bus, which is over on the south side of the building, remember?"

"Uh, Pastor?"

"Yes, Jamie?"

"I really feel like I need to go to that meeting they were talking about. Something about it ... I just really have to go to that meeting!"

I was being pulled intensely in the direction of going to Panama. It seemed so strange to feel so strongly about something I knew nothing about. My youth pastor stayed behind with me, while the rest of the people from my church climbed on the bus and left.

During the meeting, I thought back to a few months before. I had gone to a local rally at an auditorium where a man talked about Jesus Christ. He told us that Jesus Christ was someone who loved everyone. He didn't care about our past mistakes. All God wanted was a relationship with us — he wanted us to confide in him when we went through difficult times.

The man explained that God was someone who could help people out when they were having problems. He talked about prayer and how I could talk to Jesus anytime I wanted to. *I wonder if Jesus could help my family and me,* I thought.

He asked the crowd if anyone wanted to become a Christian, and since everything he had said about Jesus

New BEGINNINGS

seemed pretty nice, I stood up and walked toward the stage. Next to others who'd come up to the front alongside me, I closed my eyes.

Jesus, I want you in my heart. I want to follow what you tell me to do, and I want to live a life which is pleasing to you. When I have problems at either of my homes, I would love it if I could confide in you with what I'm feeling.

It was a moment of sweet surrender. My chest felt lighter, and the air seemed fresher.

But when I got out of the meeting, I felt very overwhelmed. I still didn't know much about how to live a Christian life or how to tell other people about Jesus.

The people in charge told me the things I would do on this trip: A dramatic play would be created and reenacted to different people in three different spots in the country of Panama. We would spend a week deep in the jungle, staying in a little village with people who lived in huts, in the inner city in Panama City, and we would visit others in a city nearby.

My heart was tugging me down a path I couldn't see. I knew my family didn't have the money to send me on this trip. To them, it probably looked like a vacation to go to Panama for a month to act out a play in front of a bunch of strangers who didn't even speak the same language as me.

Once I decided that I needed to go, though, I never thought about not going.

HOME SWEET HOME

❧❧❧

"Hello, ma'am. I'm going on a mission trip to Panama this summer, and I'm wondering if you would like to buy an egg for $1." The woman at the door stared at me, looked down at the egg I held out to her and shut the door without saying a word. *I'm not going to let this get me down,* I thought.

I walked to the next house. There wasn't anything special about the eggs, but we were selling them individually to raise money for our trip. *Every dollar counts,* I thought. I knocked on the door, a carton of eggs in one hand, a single egg in the other. An older gentleman answered the door slowly.

"Hi, sir. I'm going on a mission trip to Panama this summer, and I'm trying to raise money so that I can go. Would you like to buy an egg from me for $1 so that I can go?"

The man laughed as he glanced at the egg in my hand.

"What's a 'mission trip'?" he asked.

"It's when a bunch of people go to a different country and talk to people from that country about Jesus Christ," I explained.

"I'll tell you what — I'll give you $20 instead, is that okay?"

"Yes! Thank you so much!"

Selling eggs door-to-door, writing sponsor letters to local rich people, even asking my parents for money brought me closer and closer to my goal. I was thankful

New BEGINNINGS

when my grandparents pitched in a little money for the trip. Mom and Dad were nervous about sending their 15-year-old daughter out of the country without them, but before I left they gave me their full support. Two days before I was to leave for the trip, I was able to raise all the money I needed to go.

When I left, it was like stepping into a world I had never seen before.

Our Panama group consisted of 95 people, divided into three groups, all strangers to me. We met up in Texas for a few days to prepare. We planned on learning how to adapt in a world we'd never experienced before — poverty, dangerous animals, the jungle itself. I knew nothing of the sort. I would only be able to call my family two times during the month I was gone.

I started to feel uncomfortable.

I was anxious being around new faces in Texas. I sat by different people every day for meals, while everyone else seemed to have a friend or two who came on the trip with him or her. When we arrived in Panama, though, the situation forced us to start to rely on others in our group.

We spent a week out in the jungle, doing our play in front of the people who lived in straw huts 20 feet away from where we congregated in the makeshift church assembled from leaves and trees. That's also where my group slept each night. One unforgettable moment happened when people in my group hunted an alligator, and we ate it for supper that night.

After the week in the jungle, we traveled to a little

HOME SWEET HOME

village. One of the pastors on the trip pulled me aside. "Jamie, I'd like you to talk about your life and how you became a Christian after we do the play tonight."

"You mean, like, tell my story? I don't have a story. My parents divorced when I was 9 years old, and I've been taking care of everybody since. There isn't much else to it."

The pastor set me up with some people who could help me bring my story to life.

Wow, I actually have a story here, I thought, totally surprised by my findings.

I was completely nervous to talk about my life in front of strangers, but I was even more nervous to tell it in front of my fellow travelers and new friends.

Every time I get nervous, it's obvious to the world. I break out in hives, and my neck and face get red splotches. It's embarrassing, and since I'm already shy, public speaking terrifies me. But I believed it was important to share my story, to let others who may be going through something similar know they weren't alone. We could go through it together or at least talk about it.

After the month in Panama, we hopped on the plane back to Texas, where we spent a few days debriefing and talking about what we accomplished in Central America. Part of the debriefing process was guiding us back into life at home. Nothing about my family and problems at both of my homes was going to be any different. The transition back would be hard. I cried myself to sleep for the last couple of nights before going home.

New BEGINNINGS

This trip has made me feel at home, spending time with these people, telling stories about what you've done for me, I prayed to Jesus as I lay on my bed. *I don't even want to go home. I feel like I am home, even though I'm 1,000 miles away.*

On the trip, I learned a lot about the mysterious Jesus Christ that the man in the auditorium spoke of months prior. I discovered stories in the Bible that mirrored things I had gone through in my life being a child of divorce. I identified myself as a believer in Christ, and it felt like my life had been upgraded. I felt more positive, even despite my family troubles. Believing in God gave me the patience to understand that people are who they are, and only God can change them. I was sure that God had me where he wanted me in life and that there were reasons for the things I'd been going through.

I prayed one night in Texas, *God, even though I didn't know you most of my life, I feel like you were always there, and you brought me to this moment with you.* I couldn't see God, but I felt an overwhelming sense of comfort. Over the course of the trip, I realized I'd fallen head over heels in love with God. It was strange to think that there was someone who has always been around, who loved me and was waiting for me.

I believe God knew that when I was 15 years old, I was going to decide to become a Christian and believe in him. I understood why I had to go through bad times in my life — my bad times helped me see Jesus more clearly. He was worthy of my love because he died for me. His reasons

HOME SWEET HOME

were bigger than mine, and I learned to trust him through good times and bad. I knew that my life couldn't ever go back to the way it had been before I had Jesus in it. I knew that God was what I had been searching for to mend the brokenness that began for me when my parents divorced. I sat on my bunk and cried.

❦❦❦

Every day on the Panama trip, we had quiet time to write in a journal and read the Bible. Just a few days before we left, I read 1 Corinthians 6:17: "Whoever is united with the Lord is one with him in spirit."

I thought about it for a while.

"Well, God, that's kinda cool — it's almost as if we could be married!" I giggled thinking about it. "I mean, I don't even have *a ring*!"

Then I thought about it seriously. *I would rather be promised to you, God, than not be a Christian at all. I promise to be obedient to what the Bible tells me from now on.*

Everyone in my life was divorced. I didn't even really know what a good marriage looked like. I wanted to be faithful to God, like a wife is faithful to her husband. He had obviously always been faithful to me. Jesus deserved my devotion, and I felt sure that he would be with me when I returned home to face my troubles.

❦❦❦

New BEGINNINGS

Coming back to Ohio was definitely difficult. I was dealing with some serious reverse culture shock, and people saw the difference in me. I felt like a new person, finally ready to come out of my shell. I'd spent so long worrying and trying to create balance in my life, but now I felt free. Finally, I wasn't afraid to speak or enjoy life fully. I spent a lot of my time talking to God and reading my Bible, not wanting to revert back to the life I'd known before Panama.

A couple of weeks after coming home, it was my 16th birthday. My dad and I had discussed different things he could do for my birthday. He mentioned helping me get a job or giving me some money to go toward buying a car. My dad was wonderful when it came to giving gifts, so I really trusted that I would like whatever he chose for me.

At the dinner table, Dad placed a small bag in front of me.

"I know we talked about a couple of different things to get you for your birthday," he said, gesturing toward the bag. "I don't know how to explain this, so … just open it."

I opened the bag to find a small box inside. I lifted it out of the bag and opened it up. It looked like an engagement ring, with a gold band and a white stone in the middle.

All I could do was look at it and imagine God saying, *Here's your ring!*

"Oh! It's my wedding ring!" I exclaimed.

"What?!" my dad shouted.

My family looked at me with deep confusion.

HOME SWEET HOME

"Well, I have to tell you something about my trip to Panama." I told them the story of the night I prayed to God about the verse I'd read in my Bible and my "marriage" to him.

I'd heard people at church talk about moments where God made himself real to them. The moment I opened that ring box, I knew what they were talking about. I cried when I realized that God actually heard me when I spoke to him.

Wedding rings represented everything that had torn my life apart. They had reminded me of broken promises and battles between hurting people. But now Jesus was using the same symbol to comfort my broken heart. It was hard to understand that I was important enough to Jesus for him to listen to my prayers — that I actually mattered to him. This was how he proved it to me. I now knew what those in my youth group meant when they said that God spoke to them about something they were dealing with. It was an unbelievable feeling to have it happen to me.

From that moment on, my relationship with God felt real. It was very personal and became the most important thing in my life. I wanted to please him in everything I did and in every relationship I had.

"I want to give you everything in my life, God. It's all yours. Do with it what you will." It takes a lot to give everything of yours, not just physical things you own, but your own future to God. But I've found out that it's all worth it.

Members of my family started coming to me when

New BEGINNINGS

they were having spiritual hardships. Meeting the needs of others didn't feel like such a heavy weight on my shoulders anymore. I felt sort of privileged. I knew that God loved me unconditionally and would meet all my needs, and I was so happy to have opportunities to help others feel his love, too.

When I started dating a nice guy I met at my youth group a couple of months after my 16th birthday, I knew that he was the kind of person I could see myself *actually* marrying. Before long, I fell in love with him. I couldn't believe that I was lucky enough to find someone at such a young age, but I was also terrified of getting divorced.

When Zack asked me to marry him, I was ecstatic but also very scared. Every time we talked about the future and what we both wanted in life, we felt more sure that God had created us to be together. But I was 17 years old. To become engaged at that age had divorce written all over it. Many people had doubts that they weren't afraid to voice. I had so many conversations with Zack over time about divorce and how I never wanted it to happen to us.

"We're not even going to make 'divorce' part of our vocabulary!" he would reassure me.

"How do you know? We're not even married yet," I would retort.

Zack came from a family of people who were all still married. He didn't know what divorce was like and how common it was in my family. Divorce haunted me, even though Zack made me happier than anyone ever had. Ever since I watched the taillights of my mom's car float off in

HOME SWEET HOME

the distance when I was 9, I knew I never wanted divorce to affect the family I made for myself. Now I was in a position to actually do something about it in my own life.

☙☙☙

I gripped the porcelain sink in the bathroom and stared at the red splotches on my neck in the mirror. My white dress looked gorgeous, and the veil cascaded down over my hair in a surreal sort of way. I somehow expected my face to change now that I would soon be someone's wife. In a matter of minutes, I would have a husband. I knew Zack was the man of my dreams. I took a deep breath. I scratched my neck. The splotches weren't going away. I needed to calm down. I thought back to Panama, how I had to tell my story in front of all those people and how nervous I was then. I knew I could do it if I asked God to help me.

God, what's the matter with me? I love Zack. I just don't want to get divorced. You know my heart, and I gave it to you. Sometimes, we are deceived as people, and if this is something that you don't want me to do today, send a plane through the roof of the church or something. You need to give me a sign. I have no problem with sending everyone home if that is what you want me to do, God, I prayed quietly.

As if in response, I felt this warm, calming sensation. It was as if a blanket gently covered me. I felt immediate peace within myself. I relaxed, and the red splotches

New BEGINNINGS

disappeared. I felt like Jesus said to me, *Today you will break a generational curse.*

After that moment, I was fine. I collected myself, climbed the stairs and greeted my dad at the back of the church.

"Are you ready?" he asked.

"I sure am."

"You don't look nervous at all! You're 18 years old, about to get married and you're not scared or nervous?"

I was feeling happier than I'd ever felt before. All I could do was smile.

❧❧❧

"All right, now, give us a call when you get home so we know you're safe, okay?" I asked a friend of the family as he walked out the front door.

"Do you think that's why people come here? Because there's a sense of calm they can't find at home?" Zack asked me from the front door as we watched our friend leave. Our friend had been staying at our house, which Zack and I jokingly refer to as "the gathering place."

I thought about Zack's question. So many people long for a place to call home. My sister, Jenny, stayed with us until she graduated high school, and even Zack's brother has spent time with us in the past. In the 15 years we've been married, we've had so many opportunities to reach out to others who are going through the same things I did. It's good for them to know they're not alone.

HOME SWEET HOME

"I don't know," I said happily. "Maybe it feels like home to them. I just like that our house is known as a place people can feel welcome."

And thank you, God, for giving me what I always dreamed of, I added silently.

Our family isn't perfect. We struggle all the time, but we never give up on each other. And we always ask God to give us the opportunity to show other people what it means to have true family, whether that's in our home or in our church home at Trinity Full Gospel.

I fell in love with God when I was 15 years old, and I'm so thankful that he loves me more than anyone ever could. He had a plan for me all along. God has smoothed over so many of the rough edges from my fragmented childhood and given me a loving family and a safe place to call home.

OUT OF DEATH
The Story of Penny
Written by Holly De Herrera

    White lights pulsed above my head, and a soft hissing filled the hospital room. I tried to calm myself, snuggling the fuzzy, white bunny my brother gave me, pressing it to my nose. Dad told me to be his brave little girl, but his eyes looked watery and sad. Just a tiny hole in my heart, they said. Mom smiled in a funny way that didn't look at all like her regular smile when she talked about the "procedure." But what she didn't know is that I saw her crying behind her hands and turning away when I asked about heaven and what it's like. Just in case. I even heard the doctor say, when he thought I couldn't hear, that only three other children have lived through this. But somehow, I wasn't scared. I began to think of the room I lay in as outer space, all quiet but echoey. The doctors moved slowly and steadily around me, like astronauts getting their tools ready to take care of the repair on the itty-bitty spaceship. I thought maybe I'd float away into the sky, and who knew what I'd find?

    Later, when I'd been rolled to my recovery room, Mom told me everything. How they cut between two ribs, pulled my heart out and laid it on my chest to do the repair. The tubes hooked up like tangled fingers around my chest and face, my beating heart outside of me, attached only by the red rope of an artery. *So breakable,* I

New BEGINNINGS

thought. Just that little bit tying me to this life. But I did survive. Only the fourth patient to do so. Proof I've always been a fighter.

☙☙☙

Death can be a funny thing. It doesn't always happen all of a sudden. It can come in stages, like sand pulling away from the shoreline, pulling and pulling, giving way, until there is nothing left but rock — or, in my case, bones. Nothing left to show of what used to be except a faint outline, a vague shape. That's the way it was with me. I was once a little girl, full of dreams, full of laughter and hope for what would come, imagining myself wearing white walking down the aisle with my Prince Charming. But who I dreamed I'd be was like north and south to who I became. What I chose. It felt as if I died a slow death, little by little.

☙☙☙

Mom wasn't sure whether I'd live past my middle school years. If I did, she likely wondered whether I'd thrive. Imagining her ill child as a vibrant healthy woman was a stretch. And, if I remained ill, who would want to marry me? So, wanting a distraction for me in my youth and a way to provide for myself should I live into adulthood, she put me in piano lessons. At least that skill might prove useful should I become a spinster.

OUT OF DEATH

I loved making music. It always felt right. It wove through me, lifted my chin and made me feel like I had a purpose for being on this earth. Two years after the surgery, my soft-spoken daddy flew off, far away from us, off where people go after this life. But I ached for his gentleness. I needed his steady hand guiding me, saying, "This way. This is the way you go." But he was gone, and Mom married someone about as different from Dad as the sun is from the moon. Dad put off a light of his own. He didn't need to brag about it. He just was. But Russ, he didn't seem to have any light, and he didn't try to protect my ears like Daddy had. From what I could tell, he was just Mom's way of taking care of us since he worked and made money, and because of that, Mom could be home with us kids.

When I was 18, I fell in love with James. He had dark hair and eyes and made me feel grown up. It was his idea for us to save up for a car and then get married. He said it would take time, but it would be worth the wait because he was going into the service and had to get permission, anyway. So ours was a long-distance relationship. Phone calls each week. Love letters and promises. James said he'd found a good car, so I sent the money I earned to him and imagined him driving up in it one day and asking me to marry him. But then the letters stopped coming, and I felt a seeping inky blackness creep into the corners of my mind. *Why wasn't he writing?* I didn't understand. Then my friend dropped by and shared the news.

"Penny, James has been here for almost a week now."

New BEGINNINGS

"What, here? In town?"

"Yes."

"But, he didn't have leave. He didn't tell me."

"I'm sorry. I thought you'd want to know."

Blasts of anger fired in my mind, overlapping, tumbling over each other. *Why didn't he tell me?* Even though physically my heart no longer gave me trouble, something inside, in a far back corner, seemed to tear — a slow bleeding out.

I went to his house and waited on his front porch until he arrived. He pulled up in a car, clearly the one he bought using the money I sent. The sound of his tires squealing to a stop on the brick street grated on my nerves. When he took the steps onto the porch, he looked everywhere but at my eyes.

"What's going on, James? Why didn't you tell me you were home? Why haven't you written?" I crossed my arms over my chest like that would help.

He chanced a glance at my face. "Didn't you get my letter?"

"Letter? What letter? You've sent me lots of letters, except for in this last month."

"I wrote you. I told you I couldn't keep going like this." His tone accused rather than apologized.

Forcing my voice to remain steady, I took in a slow, even breath. "I got no letter, James."

"Oh. Well, I wrote. I told you. It's not my fault you didn't get it."

"What else did you say? Why can't we be together?

OUT OF DEATH

Did you meet someone else?" My thoughts scattered to all the calls, the meaningless words he'd said to me.

Digging his hands into his pockets, he began, "Susan is nice. She lives near base and …"

"But we were going to get married. You — we bought a car!" My argument sounded lame even to me. Is that all I really had? Such a tiny thread holding me to him? Did he even love me? Did I?

"I know. I just can't now. I love Susan."

"But not me."

Silence.

"How long?"

At this he looked up at me. Finally. "How long, what?"

"How long have you been with her?"

"Several months."

"We were still talking on the phone several months ago." I hated the whine in my voice and the wavering way my words came out. I refused to cry, so I just swallowed, over and over. Fists opening and closing, I asked because I had to know. "Was she there those times when we talked? When you pretended you cared about me?"

A small nod was all he offered, but it was enough.

Nauseated, I turned away to keep him from seeing that I cared at all. But since it was already too late for that, I just turned and stalked toward the stupid vehicle.

"Please just take me home."

The ride home was all silence and engine. I wanted to take a bat and smash in the dashboard, the hood, the windows; instead, I just sat there like a statue. At home, I

New BEGINNINGS

walked up the porch steps and opened the front door. When I turned around, all that was left were the blood-red taillights getting smaller and smaller, until the night sky simply swallowed them up. It was as if I finally saw my life for what it was: a see-through, depression-glass façade. And it took nearly nothing to shatter it.

After that I was on the hunt. I wouldn't let James or anyone else watching know that I had lost anything. Nobody was going to have that kind of power over me. So I put the money I had saved into a 1956 Ford Convertible. I was a secretary, and I had plans for my future, and none of it included being needy or weak.

Life took on a new rhythm. I spent a lot of time at the service station getting my car or my stepdad's car worked on. That's when I met Brian. At first, we were just friends. It felt good to be around him and laugh and talk while he worked. Besides, he was married and 18 years older than me, and it was nice knowing there weren't any expectations. One night after dinner when I was relaxing in the family room, the phone rang. My stepdad got up to answer it and just stood there, then hung up. Again the phone rang, and again he hung it up.

"What was that all about?" Mom asked.

"No idea. Some crazy woman yelling all sorts of names."

"Like what?"

"Whore." He looked over at my mom and then at me, and then we all started laughing.

It happened several more times that night.

OUT OF DEATH

The next day Russ was down at the station telling Brian about it, and that's when we found out that the woman was Brian's wife who was jealous of me being around him. Brian told him that she was crazy, they had been separated and he was trying to finalize the divorce, but in the meantime, she wouldn't let up. That she did this any time he made friends.

It's funny, but that's when I started to actually notice Brian. Watched how his body looked as he leaned into a vehicle or how his mouth moved when he smiled. It was then that I realized that his wife had every reason not to trust me because I wanted what she had. And I justified it because they were separated and Brian had already decided to leave her. It didn't matter to me that he was older than I was; that only added to the excitement of it all.

So we started meeting, late at night, at his trailer out in the middle of nowhere. I spent many nights there alone with him. I felt awakened and alive and in control. And I just knew that once Brian's divorce was final that we would be together and be happy and never worry or fight. Brian would be able to introduce me to his friends as the woman he loved.

Our love affair went on for more than a year and was always the same. Meet late, knock on the door of his silver Airstream, step into the dark trailer and live out our fantasies together. Everything was perfect. Except that I kept asking when we would be getting married, and even after the divorce was final, he just kept saying, "I'm not getting married again. Besides, you're too young, Penny. I'm an old man compared to you."

"I don't care about that. You know that!"

"But I care. You have your life ahead of you. I have kids. I can't marry you."

I'd pull away, but it was always too dark to really let him see my face, the disappointment I hoped would hurt him.

"But that doesn't mean we can't still be together. Like this." His arms wrapped me up in the black of the small space, and even then I knew it was all for nothing. The high I got being near him, being with him, lasted only until the moment it ended, and all that was left was a growing pit full of regret.

It had been several weeks since we'd been together, and I felt I might scream in frustration if it lasted much longer. So I decided to stop by the station just as Brian would be getting off work. Night had set in, slinking in the unlit spaces. Walking up, I saw him there with someone else looking on longingly. I had seen her before, but now I stopped to really watch, and it was as though I was observing myself there, eyes adoring, smile teasing. And Brian did the same. Slowly, steadily, I walked forward, breathing in through my nose, out through my mouth.

"Brian, can we talk?" I flicked a glance at the woman who now looked nothing like me closer up. She looked older, presentable and maybe even nice. I felt certain she wasn't a slut, either. A sour taste crept up my throat knowing what was happening. Again.

OUT OF DEATH

Away from the woman, he began, "We were high school sweethearts." Like that explained everything. "She's my age and has two kids of her own."

I just stood there, rooted to the ground like my toes had become claws holding on for dear life to a ridiculously small branch.

"Penny, you and me, it was fun while it lasted. But we both knew that wasn't forever. I always told you we couldn't get married."

I almost laughed out loud knowing what he said was true. I had been nothing but momentary entertainment, an intermission between two acts. And I had unwittingly set it up that way.

It was almost as though something took over my body as I turned and left. Something got me in that car, and something turned the ignition and drove away. I found myself on Route 60, nothing but darkness and a long, grey stretch of road in front of me. No beacons. No streetlights. Just darkness. I felt so empty and worthless that I just wanted to plunge into the void and disappear. *Poof.* Be gone and done with.

I pressed my foot on the gas and heard the engine getting louder and louder. *Maybe,* I thought, *if I went fast enough, I would dive right off the end of the world, and then the ache I tried so hard to ignore would just go away.* My foot pushed down on the pedal, down to the floor, the night whipping past. It all looked the same, it was so empty out there. But that's when I thought of my sister and my mom. *What would they do if I died? How would*

New BEGINNINGS

they manage? My foot let up just a little, and the car seemed to sigh and stop roaring so loud. *And what if I didn't die but ended up just crippled and pitiful?* My foot relaxed more. The rapid beating of my heart slowed, and I stared forward, my headlights illuminating only the 20 feet in front of me, nothing else. I couldn't see anything but that and the ghostly way my hands gripped the steering wheel in front of me. Somehow I got home, stepped into the quiet of my house, made my way to my bedroom and curled into a tight ball and slept.

☙☙☙

    Being the lonely, solitary girl didn't suit me. I wanted to be loved. I needed to be held. But I wasn't going to wait around to be found. I heard that Red, a boy I had liked in high school, had moved back to Adamsville, and that got me hunting again. There was a square dance going on one night, and I thought he might be there, so I showed up and pretended to be surprised when he walked up to me.

    "Red, it's so good to see you here." I offered my sweetest smile.

    "Same to you." He stood tall and lanky, but I could tell by the way his arms filled out his plaid button-up shirt that he had grown into a strong man, too. Besides, I knew he threw hay bales, and that took some muscle. He stood with one foot slightly out in front of the other, like he meant to relax and talk a while. His red hair nearly glowed, it was so striking against his pale skin. I guessed from the way his blue eyes took me in that he might just suspect that I had sought him out.

I actually felt giddy seeing him there. And I couldn't believe I could be giddy about anything anymore, being such a woman of the world. Having experienced passion with a man nearly twice my age. But I pretended to be the kind of girl Red would want to be with. Sweet. Innocent. We started dating after that meeting, and before I knew it, I was in love. He was nothing like Brian. He was kind and smiled easily and knew what he wanted in life. He was a gentleman and asked nothing from me that didn't belong to him. We even went to church together, and a sense that this was what real love felt like, what a good relationship felt like, settled over me. One Saturday afternoon he pulled up to the local church and turned in the driver's seat and said, "Wait here, okay?"

"Sure. Okay." I relaxed my head back and watched him run through the parking lot. What happened next seemed like a dream, or maybe the living out of my nightmares. Out the front of the church ran the newlyweds, Brian and the woman from the service station. They both smiled as rice was thrown in their direction from happy friends and family. She made the perfect bride. She wore white, and Brian held her hand like she was all he had ever wanted. I slid down in my seat trying not to cry, swallowing against the thickness in my throat. I stayed that way until Red opened the door, giving me a sidelong glance before turning his full attention to me.

With strong hands he reached for me. "Penny." He

New BEGINNINGS

looked down at my fingers, bare and reaching outward, palms curled in like tulips. Then he looked up. "Will you marry me?"

Everything that only moments ago had swirled around me like a swarm of bees seemed to calm. The hum of regret quieted. I sat up straight in my seat and said without any doubt or fear, "Yes." This was right. No sneaking in the dark involved. Just two people in love, living out their dreams in the full light of day. I hadn't even realized he'd run through the parking lot and down the street to the local jewelry store.

We set the date for July the 5th, a holiday weekend. We couldn't do a honeymoon right away because both of us had to work, but neither of us cared. We were in love, and it didn't matter.

༺༺༺

My brother, Less, liked to commune with the dead, and he held séances at the kitchen table, transforming it into something ugly and cold instead of where we ate pancakes and talked about the news. He saw no harm in it, but it made me afraid to be alone, to go to bed at night.

One night, after all of Less' friends had gone, I lay in bed trying to get some sleep since I had to work the next morning. I felt the air in the room change. It felt thick with static.

My body tingled, and I thought I saw something black and fluxing move toward me, from the foot of my bed to

OUT OF DEATH

the side. A dark figure that seemed larger than me, stronger. My head throbbed, and my throat seemed to close. I couldn't get any words out to call for my mom, to scream for help. A cool sweat spread across my chest as I tightened my fists on the blankets spread over my body. The darkness pulsed beside me, like it was studying me, leaning in to me, drawing my breath out of my throat. Finally I said it, quiet at first and then screaming, "Mom! Help! Mom!"

And instantaneously the mass shot out the window and into the night. Gone. And I didn't know if it was ever really there or if I was crazy or if evil was real and ready to take over at any minute. Or if it had already gotten in me somehow.

☙☙☙

Two nights before the wedding, Red and I met after his shift at work. Pulling up to the drive-in late that night, he asked, "What would my bride like to eat?"

"A burger, fries and a Coke, please."

He grinned at me and put in our order. After eating, we drove out to the farmhouse we had been offered by Red's dad, free of charge our first year of marriage. All of our new furniture had already been delivered, but we wanted to set things up our own way so that when we went home after the wedding, everything would be just right.

"Why don't we get things set for breakfast so that it

New BEGINNINGS

will be easy to eat together before going to work the morning after we get married?" I smiled thinking about being together in our home. It was as though I had been given a do-over. A chance to have the life I'd always wanted.

"Great idea." Red looked up at me and grinned, lingering a little too long.

"What?"

"You know what."

"No, I don't," I lied.

"Mmm-hmm."

I felt the heat creep up my cheeks. Red and I had done things right, saving ourselves for after the "I do." And because of that, I just knew our wedding night would be the most beautiful moment of my life. It would be ours and only ours.

"All right. Let's get this done. Stop flirting," I told him.

He reached across and grabbed the silverware, keeping eye contact and then, without another word, carefully placed the utensils beside our plates.

It was 2 a.m. by the time he dropped me off at my house, crickets sawing legs together and fireflies flashing on and off softly around us. "Why don't you just come home with me? You could stay in the spare room."

"No, it's bad luck for you to see the bride the day before the wedding."

"I have some news for you. It *is* the day before the wedding."

"Well, not to me, since I haven't gone to sleep yet."

OUT OF DEATH

"Oh, is that how it works?"

"Yes, besides I'm getting my hair permed in the morning, and I need to be there early."

"Okay. If you're sure." Red leaned in and brushed his lips against mine, like a butterfly landing and taking off too soon. "Love you."

"Love you, too."

And he turned and walked down the path to his car, the dark night swallowing up his tall body.

The next morning, a knock woke me. Insistent and urgent, it continued, and I was worried my stepdad would wake up so I stumbled down the stairs and opened the front door. An officer stood there, legs spread, hands in front of him holding something.

"Do you know Ben Wagner?"

"Enough to marry him tomorrow."

The officer cleared his throat, then said, "Did you see him last night?"

I wondered if Red had gotten in some kind of trouble, and my mind spun wondering how to answer. "Yes. We went for dinner, then spent a few hours setting up our furniture so it would be ready after the wedding and then he dropped me off here. Why?"

"What time did he leave here?"

"Around 2. I'm not sure. Why? What's wrong?"

"There was an accident."

"Was he hurt? Where was it?"

"Adamsville Road."

My heart felt like it was beating in slow motion but

heavy and painful. "How badly hurt? Is he in the hospital?"

The officer shifted again. "No. He's dead."

He said something about him driving over the center line, swerving behind some people also out driving late, something about him being drunk, and I answered no, we had a Coke and burger and fries and we had been setting up furniture, and it couldn't be Red because we were getting married tomorrow. But it seemed the truth couldn't be avoided: He simply fell asleep and would never wake up. His car wrapped around a tree and caught on fire. They said he would have died instantly. They said arrangements would need to be made. They said no open casket because he was no longer recognizable.

☙ ☙ ☙

The furniture stores agreed to take back everything, no charge. And the flowers we had planned for our wedding were instead spread all over the church for Red's funeral. Our breakfast plates were stacked and put away and the house put up for rent. But even with all the preparations, nothing felt real. *How could this have happened?* I did everything right this time. I tried so hard to remember what a good girl should do. How one should act. And I had loved Red. But now a spreading, deepening loneliness dug into me, like roots of a weed sending out runners, sending out ground cover. I wanted to hide, be anywhere but there watching them lower Red's body into the ground, watching them shoveling dirt on his body that just days before had been near me, warm and alive and laughing. Nothing made sense. I felt cursed and hollow.

Gripping the small white Bible meant to be in my hands as I walked down the aisle to my groom, I sat on an uncomfortable folding chair set up beside the burial site. Everyone left or lingered in the background, whispering like it mattered. Like anyone here could listen to the words, anyway. No, it was all so pointless. Trying to be good. Trying to love and give and hope. Whispering when nobody heard once the light had been extinguished. Tears clogged up against the back of my eyes and the back of my throat, but I swallowed hard, blinked and squeezed my eyes shut. Nothing would make me cry. Nothing would hurt me ever again. I stood slowly, hearing the creak of the seat and vaguely registering the pastor and his wife on the periphery of my view. And I set it down on the coffin. The Bible. What was I going to do with it, anyway? It had been meant for another girl. One who was going to be happy and good. One whose dreams had finally come true.

Then the pastor's wife, Suzanne, stepped forward. "Penny, you don't want to do that now, do you really?" Her voice was soft and entreating, but it irritated me nonetheless.

"Yes. Yes, I do. I don't need it anymore." That small rectangle of white seemed so out of place against the blackish-brown of the dirt surrounding Red's coffin and scattered on top. But it represented something to me. A letting go, a leaving behind — because that part of me felt

New BEGINNINGS

dead, too. Because holding onto it would only remind me of what I had come so close to having. *Besides, God obviously didn't want me to be happy,* I concluded, *so what good would it do?*

Walking away from Red's grave, I only heard the quiet sigh of the pastor's wife and the words, "Oh, Penny …"

❧❧❧

Six months later, I married a loser. I knew it minutes into the ceremony. *This isn't right! This won't be good! Don't do it!* But who was I to listen to *me*, anyway? I had been wrong so many times before, and besides, I needed someone warm in my bed at night. The loneliness had burrowed deeper, and I knew I needed help pretending like I wasn't half dead inside. A year later, my baby boy was born, and he made it all worth it. His life proved that I had something good to give, something worth living for. But Jack couldn't handle life, let alone being a dad and husband, and only two years after we said, "I do," I realized I couldn't. So I dropped him off at the Y and said, "Goodbye."

❧❧❧

Somehow Brian stepped back into my life. He told me that his marriage was a mess and that if he didn't get out of it he was going to kill her. He even confessed to grinding up rat poison and putting it in her special hypoallergenic lotion. But that didn't ring a bell that he wasn't someone to get involved with again. Neither had the way he'd treated me before been a clue. I just needed to be touched. It didn't matter much to me that there was no future. I just remembered feeling alive and excited with him and needed that again.

"Meet me tonight?"

"Yeah, I'll be there."

"Same time?"

"Yes. Late."

So I'd drive out to the silver trailer, ironically shaped like a bullet, and we would pretend we both could actually love another human being.

Only it was a lie, just like it had been before. It didn't take long for me to see this time that he would never, ever marry me, would never treat me like Red had. He just wanted the late-night meetings with nothing offered in exchange. And even though that had been okay with me at first, it didn't last. Whenever we were together, I felt the chasm inside me widening, gaping with emptiness. The passion lasted minutes, and when it was over, I felt dirtier and more alone than ever.

"Do you think we might get married? Someday? I could make you happy. See how happy I make you?" I couldn't see, just heard my own voice practically begging in the shadowy trailer. I hated how pathetic it made me sound, but I had to ask.

"No, you know I don't want to get married again."

"Yeah, you said that once before, too, and look what happened."

New BEGINNINGS

"But not again. I know that now."

And the quiet spread out between us like an empty warehouse full of nothing.

I worked at a factory at the first-aid station, bandaging the workers who got injured on the job. It wasn't thrilling, but it paid the bills. Sandy started coming around regularly, smiling and tucking her hair behind her ear, her cheeks growing rosy when we talked. Complimenting me. Making me think that maybe I was beautiful.

"That yellow outfit makes you look sexy, you know?"

"It does?" I smoothed down the creases and grinned. "No, I did not know that!" I giggled, feeling light and pretty for once. Brian was an idiot and had no clue what he was giving up. So maybe I didn't need to wait around for him to come to his senses.

Sandy visited me at my house, and we began hanging out, talking. I felt different with her, like she saw me as more than just a thing to use, someone important and desirable.

It didn't take long for me to decide. Whether it seemed natural or not, I'd seen that nothing works out how you might expect, and sometimes you just have to take hold of what is right in front of you, begging for your attention and love. And so I did. Sandy moved in, and nobody knew that we weren't just roommates. Nobody knew that we were lovers.

But in time the drama of life with Sandy got to be too much. She packed her bags and pictures, screaming that she was leaving practically every week, and I got so tired of running after her, begging her to stay. Besides, she never lifted a finger to pay the bills and expected me to carry the whole load on my own. The one-sidedness of this began to resemble how things had been with Brian, and so I decided I'd had enough.

Anna stepped into the picture around this time, and I was enamored with her, the feminine way she carried herself and the class she displayed in her interactions. She treated me in a way I hadn't experienced with anyone except Red, and I saw this as my chance for a new beginning.

She became my everything, but still I felt empty. The hollowness seemed enormous and impossible to fill with any amount of love. Around this time my sister, Betsy, "found Jesus" and began her crusade to "save my soul."

"You know you're not living right, Penny. Why don't you consider coming to church with me? Check it out. At least see what you think."

But I couldn't bear the thought because everything I had chosen stood in opposition to a life of holiness, and I felt too dirty to even consider it. But my sister wouldn't give up. Daily she called me, left messages for me, encouraged me to just try and see what might happen. Only I knew what would happen. I would come face to face with myself, and I couldn't bear the thought. Betsy watched my son, though, and I had no choice but to keep my relationship with her from falling apart. I needed her. Anyway, she was my sister and had a right to drive me crazy.

New BEGINNINGS

"Penny, God loves you. He longs for you to come to him and open your heart to him."

"Betsy, I just can't. I'm afraid. I would lose Anna. I can't bear to hurt her."

"I see."

"I doubt you do."

And so the conversations repeated over and over until I felt I couldn't stand to even answer the phone, knowing it was most likely my sister pestering me again.

But that didn't change the loneliness. It didn't change the ache. The days when Betsy had my son, I would drive the long trek to her house to get him, and in the dark and quiet of my car I would sob, call out my suffering and tell God that I wanted to have him in my life, but I just couldn't hand it over. I was so full of darkness and so enmeshed in it that I saw no exit plan. The pain increased over time, and things got awkward with Anna because I didn't want to live that way anymore with her, but I saw no way out. The drives to get my son became the only times I could say how I really felt, and strange as it sounds, I felt God just might be in the passenger seat listening to me cry out to the night sky.

One night I perceived a dark mass in my car and, just like before, felt it swoop out my window. But this time was different. I felt something leave me. Maybe I was just imagining it, or maybe something else caused it, but I changed that day, and I felt like something broke off of me. Like a huge boulder lifted off my shoulders and somehow the inexplicable happened. I no longer desired

Anna. She was my friend, no more — someone I still loved but not in the same way. I felt such a deep guilt, like I had pulled her into my darkness and was going to have to leave her there. That only made me feel more alone and alien than ever. It was like I didn't belong anywhere.

Anna saw the shift in me and tried to draw me out.

"What's going on, Penny?"

"Nothing. Nothing's going on."

"Really? Because you seem different. Far away."

"I don't know what you're talking about." *What were lies after everything else I'd done?*

"Hmm."

"I'm serious. I'm just tired, I guess."

"You're always tired lately."

And I was, deep down. So terribly, terribly tired.

Betsy kept calling, inviting me to her church, telling me that it didn't mean I was committing to anything. That I was just being open and didn't I believe in that, anyway?

One evening she called when I was busy painting the home Anna and I were renting to get it ready for our move. "Penny, could you come to church tomorrow morning? It would make me so happy if you would join me."

"No, I don't think so. I'm painting and just need to finish."

"Finish tonight, and come tomorrow then."

"We'll see."

"Penny?"

"What?"

New BEGINNINGS

"I feel like it's important. Like you're running out of time to make a decision."

"What's that supposed to mean?"

"I just feel you need to really think about it because eventually it will be too late."

"Nice. Scaring me into going to church."

"I'm not trying to do that. I just feel like by saying no over and over again, you're steeling your heart, and I think you really need to be willing to think about it, not just say no again without realizing what it means."

"What does it mean?"

"It means you're making your choice."

After hanging up the phone, I stared out the upstairs bedroom window, watching the slate-grey sky swirling like a Van Gogh painting. The trees swayed and sagged against the sky, and clouds raced across like they were fleeing from something. I wondered how I could bear to decide between my life and God. Fear crept up and reminded me that someone who had lived a life like I had would probably never be accepted by God. It just didn't line up with everything I had heard about him. I turned away from the window.

The next morning I didn't go to church with my sister. And a terrible rock settled in my stomach. My life felt like a dead-end street, and somehow I had chosen to miss the only bus out. Cornered, I simply kept trying to find my way out. But nothing seemed like it would help. My mess had gotten out of control and reached its webbed fingers throughout my whole life.

OUT OF DEATH

Early the next morning, I received another call from Betsy. "Penny, you didn't come this morning."

"No. I was painting so late, I just couldn't get up this morning." The truth was I hadn't slept well. My fear and panic that I was missing out on my only lifeline kept replaying itself, though I couldn't make myself just get up and go to church.

"Well, there's a gospel music group coming to church tonight. I thought you might like to come hear them sing. I know how much you love music."

I paused, feeling like I could handle this. Maybe going to see some music group wasn't such a big deal, and then I could see what all of the fuss was about and whether my last hope really could be found there. "Well, maybe."

"Think about it, sister." She stopped as though thinking. "I really would love for you to come."

Swallowing past my emotion, I said, noncommittally, "Okay. Maybe I'll see you there."

Something pulled me to the church, and because it seemed like this was something that just wouldn't quit badgering me, I decided to go all out and invite Anna to go, too. If I was going to have a life-changing experience, she might as well be there to witness it so I'd have less explaining to do later. Sitting in the service, I felt a sense that I was meant to be there. That God really had been wooing me all along, mainly in the privacy of my car on those long drives to get my son from Betsy's house. Comfort and warmth covered me as I realized when I made those journeys, I hadn't been alone. God's spirit had

New BEGINNINGS

been there, too, talking me off the ledge and reminding me that he was there to listen and love me when I had felt least lovable.

After the sermon, the pastor called out an invitation. "If any of you wants to give his or her life to the Lord, come forward now. Don't wait."

The old stubbornness kept me pinned to the seat, even though my insides screamed out for me to quit being such an idiot. *Go up there! What are you waiting for? Your life is a mess, what do you have to lose?*

But I couldn't move. That's when I felt it. Anna's hand squeezing mine. Looking over into her pale green eyes brimming with tears like her entire insides were drowning and I was only now seeing the levels rise. I was only just now seeing the agony she had lived with, too. "Do you want to go up?" She looked so small and vulnerable but so hopeful, too.

I nodded and jumped out of my seat, Anna following closely. Before I even made it to the end of the row, Betsy grabbed my arms. "Please don't leave, Penny. Please!"

I pulled her to my chest and spoke in her ear. "I'm not, sister. We're going up to give our lives to Jesus."

Tears seemed to gush from my sister's face then, and instead of holding me, she practically shoved me toward the front of the church. And at that moment, walking forward, one foot in front of the other, I knew that the living God, the same one who made the heavens and the earth, was waiting, had been patiently waiting all along, full of love and forgiveness, for me. Nothing in my life prepared me for that moment. No relationship. No passion. Nothing could have helped me see the unconditional love that I now believed God had for me all along. He was the patient groom waiting for me to come to him. He had held my hand in the darkness. Held me as I had cried myself to sleep night after night. Waiting for me to let go and choose him.

An image of myself as a little girl came to mind, my heart lying on my chest, being mended, the small hole being carefully closed. It seemed kind of like that again. I was being healed from the inside out, and life and joy waited for me on the other side of the surgery God needed to perform.

༺༻༺༻༺༻

Life changed dramatically for both Anna and me after that day. We both felt new and whole, washed clean in the full light of day. The old guilt was gone, and freedom soaked in, seeped into every hidden corner now exposed and healing. Miraculously, Sandy soon gave her life to Jesus, too. It was as if all the broken pieces, all the casualties of my choices were being pulled back in and made new.

I moved to Zanesville and dove into life at Trinity Full Gospel Church. Teaching Sunday school and helping out with music took much of my free time, especially with a church building project going on, too. One afternoon, about six years after my life changed completely, I was at

New BEGINNINGS

the new building trying to get the bulletins ready to print. I went looking for the pastor, who was in the sanctuary helping nail something to something else. The unusual lull in the pounding ushered me into the room, strewn with two-by-fours and power tools. I walked in and spotted him, but he was standing near a man who was seated on a pile of wood eating his lunch.

"Penny, I'd like you to meet Troy. He's our contractor and came in to help."

I turned my attention to the man. Even though he was sitting, I could tell he was about my height. He wore paint-stained work trousers and a button-up shirt and sat with his elbows on his knees eating his lunch.

"Hi, nice to meet you. I'm Penny." *Didn't Pastor just give my name?* "I do the bulletins." *Impressed?* During the exchange that I seemed to be having more with myself than him, he just looked on with a pleasant smile on his face. Like I amused him or I had something weird on my face.

"Nice to meet you, Penny. I've heard all about you from your pastor."

"Oh." I certainly hoped not. Nothing could be worse.

"Well, I better get going." He stood to go, and I mentally confirmed, *Yep, near my height and nice-looking, too.*

"Yes, sir, don't want to be late for the wife." The pastor laughed for some unknown reason and punched Troy lightly on the arm.

"No, don't want to keep her waiting." He grinned and

then chuckled as he gathered his things. I liked his smile and the easy way he talked.

Not really understanding the exchange, I turned and left, completely forgetting the point of my trip over but leaving with the distinct impression that I had just missed out on an inside joke. I was also thinking that this man must be a good one considering that he cared enough to go home at a decent time to his wife. *Not many men like that anymore,* I thought.

Troy was around more and more and started attending meetings and services, so I saw him often, but never with his wife.

"I caught him looking at you. When you were playing the organ the other day." Anna raised her eyebrows at the scowl I offered.

"What? That doesn't mean anything. Everyone looks that way when the music starts."

"But not just then. I've seen him watching you other times."

"Well, that's just sick and wrong."

Sandy grinned and tipped her head toward mine. "Why? He's a man, isn't he?"

"Yes, but a married one."

Silence.

"I didn't see a ring." Sandy widened her eyes as if the comment were as innocent as mentioning the time.

"So?"

"Well, he might not be." Anna leaned back in her chair looking smug and comfortable.

New BEGINNINGS

"Or he might not wear it so he can eye innocent women." I stopped myself then. "And then not look like a jerk."

"Or he just might not be married," Sandy nearly whined.

And the teasing increased so that I could almost not stand to be near Troy. I didn't want anything to do with that kind of life ever again. Affairs and intrigue had been less intriguing than one might think, and the whole business made me feel sick to my stomach. No, if God wanted me to marry again, he'd have to literally drop the man in front of me and speak in an audible voice, preferably in King James English.

The building project had caused my pastor major back pain since he spent nearly every waking minute pounding nails into wood or sawing something. One afternoon I was in helping again, and I saw him reach and grab at his lower back, hunching slightly, and even though he was turned away from me, I could almost see the look of pain on his face. I ran over and took the hammer he was holding in his right hand.

"Go home."

"No, I just have this one thing to finish up."

"Don't make me get bossy."

"Too late." He managed a weak smile.

"I can do this."

"It involves nailing up wood while on the ladder."

"And?"

"And I'll just finish it up, then go."

OUT OF DEATH

I stood there like I was a wall instead of a woman. Seeing I wasn't going to back down, he lowered his shoulders even more and turned to go. He managed to mumble a "thanks" on his way out.

Now what? I thought. Snatching up a box of nails, I started climbing the ladder set up against the wall.

"Need some help?" Troy walked from the back of the room with a knowing grin on his face.

"No, I'm perfectly capable, thanks."

"Well, I know you are, but it can be hard to hold a two-by-four up, then nail it without someone on the other end."

Seeing I did actually need him annoyed me, but I conceded, thinking my pastor would be mad if I kicked him out but didn't get his work done. "Fine."

He jogged back to grab another ladder, then set it up a few feet down the wall near mine. "Ready?"

He held one end of the piece of wood and looked at me expectantly, a little challenge in his eyes.

"Yep." I snatched up my end and began climbing, not worrying whether I was going at the same rate he was in my movements. We worked alongside each other, and I began to relax as we talked and hammered wood. Besides, maybe Anna and Sandy were wrong, and I had been mad at the man for no good reason. I felt my body relax some and found myself actually having fun.

At church that weekend, Pastor managed to work Troy into his sermon about integrity. I gave a private sniff, thinking, *Yeah, right!* quickly scolding myself once again.

New BEGINNINGS

Then Pastor said that Troy was 50 and had never been married! *What?* I didn't understand. *Didn't they say he had to go home to his wife?* I turned and watched his profile, wondering how I could have misunderstood and shifting my opinion around like one of those puzzles with square tiles. Things started to make more sense, but still, some of it didn't go together the way I had thought.

"He's not married, eh?" Anna leaned in. "You know what that means, don't you?"

"What? What does it mean?"

"It means I was right and you were wrong."

I felt my face get hot. "Nope."

"Nope what?"

"Nope. You're not right."

"Okay, then. We'll see."

I pretended to be busy looking up scripture in my Bible but only saw Troy in my mind. Slow, steady, soft-spoken Troy, whose smile set me at ease and awakened me at the same time.

Several weeks went by, but my awareness of Troy's every move started getting on my own nerves. *What am I, a teenager?* At 42, I had no excuse for being so flighty.

One Sunday evening, after the service, several of my friends and I lingered in the church sanctuary, talking about our plans for the week and catching up on each other's news.

Troy was nearby, and I could almost feel him waiting for a chance to talk to me alone. When everyone started moving out of the pews, he leaned forward and spoke quietly. "Penny, would you like to go get some pizza or something?"

I shook my head and said, "No, I'm sorry. I really need to work on the Hallelujah chorus. It's really hard, and I want to be ready."

He looked down quickly, then up again and said, "All right. Well, talk to you later then."

"Bye." I watched his back as he left and felt like screaming at myself. That evening I spent hours working through the piece of music that I had used as an excuse. I took my frustration out on the organ.

Troy asked me out again, and I gave some other lame excuse. Ever the gentleman, he simply nodded and left.

A few weeks later, I felt this pressing need to talk to Troy but just couldn't get up the nerve. Instead, I spent the entire church service pacing the square-shaped halls like I was training for a marathon.

My sister stopped me. "What's up with you?"

"I'm running."

"From whom?"

"Troy."

"Well, why on earth would you do that?"

"Because I know he's going to ask me out."

"So? What's wrong with that?"

"Because I told God that if he wanted me to get married again, he would have to drop a man right in front of me."

"And don't you think that's what he's doing?" Betsy leaned into me and raised her eyebrows, waiting.

New BEGINNINGS

"Hmm …"

"Yeah, hmm is right." She turned to go.

Heart thumping and palms sweating, I entered the sanctuary, knowing he was there and wondering how I could approach him without seeming deranged. But he spotted me and moved forward. "Penny, hi."

"Hi." My mouth felt suddenly pasty, and words eluded me.

"I wondered." He looked out over my shoulder, then down at his hands, then back up to my face. "I wondered if I could take you out for dinner."

Before I changed my mind, I said yes in a desperate, I-was-waiting-for-you-to-ask-me-out sort of way. "I mean, yes, I'd love to go."

As if he had expected another rejection, his face changed from stoic to elated in seconds. An enormous grin on his face, he turned and started running toward the door, then stopped and said, "I'll bring the truck around!"

He jogged off, and I called his name. He stopped and turned, and I said, "Don't bring it in here, okay?"

He let out a breath and laughed. "All right. I won't." Then he left, and that was the beginning of many dates that led to many long talks. Then came the day when he asked me to marry him, and all I could say was yes.

But the joy felt so fragile, and Troy still didn't know about my past. I didn't know what to do, thinking I could lose him, I could lose everything if I said what I'd done, who I was. But I decided that if I wasn't going to slink back into the shadows, I had to be honest and live with the

OUT OF DEATH

outcome. Hiding the truth from him felt a worse possibility than him choosing to say goodbye.

One afternoon we were out driving, and I said, "Would you mind if we talked?"

He looked over his shoulder at me and said, "Sure."

Pulling over to the side of the road, then turning off the engine, he waited quietly for me to begin.

And I did. I poured out the truth of my life, tears and words tumbling out. The truth about what I'd done and how I'd lived. At first, he didn't say anything, just sat there looking down at some distant thought, maybe imagining the horrible things I'd shared. The waiting felt agonizing, and I just knew he was thinking through how to dump me in a gentlemanly way when he interrupted my thoughts. "Penny, did Jesus forgive you?" I nodded, a lump clogging my throat and tears threatening. "Well, then, who am I not to?"

It was that simple and that beautiful. His forgiveness was the most loving act I had ever experienced, and I knew it was only because of Christ that my future husband could do such a thing.

ತಿ*ತಿ*ತಿ*

A few years before Troy and I got married, I received a call.

"Penny? This is Meg. Do you remember my parents? My dad was the pastor at your church and attended at the funeral for Red?"

New BEGINNINGS

The Bible. That was all I could think of. The Bible on top of Red's casket. How I had regretted that decision. How I wished I could take it back. As calm as I could, I answered, "Yes. I remember."

"Oh, well, Mom's in town and asked me to call and see if she could stop by. She wanted to talk with you."

I couldn't imagine what she could want with me. Maybe she wanted to tell me how big a mistake I had made or to see how I turned out after turning my back on God. When Suzanne walked in a few days later, though, she had a smile stretched across her face, and her eyes seemed to hold some hidden mischief. She began without preamble. "I have something for you." She reached in her purse and pulled out the small white Bible I had laid on Red's coffin.

"But it's been 25 years."

"I know, but I just couldn't let it be buried. I knew I needed to save it for you. I prayed so much over the years for you to turn back to Jesus, and then I'd give it back. Because I just knew you'd want it."

"Oh, thank you. I did want it. I do!" I touched the soft cover, feeling the letters etched in gold, knowing I would forever look at it and remember how God had pulled me out of the grave, too.

❧❧❧

A lot of things have changed over the years. But the good things are the same. We are still a bunch of imperfect but saved people in desperate need of a Savior, doing our best to be real and reach out with real hands to any person walking through our doors.

Troy and I have been married now for more than three decades, and he has never used my past against me. He simply loves me as I am, a new and whole woman. Even to this day when he walks by my Sunday school classroom, I still get a little tickle in my chest and say, "There he goes." Because he is my gift. He is the reward I didn't deserve. And it's all because God took me out of death and into life.

HOUSES, HOME AND HARMONY
The Story of Caroline
Written by Arlene Showalter

"That's it," Truman stated, crossing his arms.

"What?" I feigned innocence.

"You know *what*. I won't stay around and watch you self-destruct. You have so much to live for, and look at you." He waved an arm to include the machines that bleeped around me and the IV line that dripped life into me.

"Either you stop or I'm outta here."

☙☙☙

My entire extended family could fit into a nine-passenger van. As my sister and I were the only grandchildren on either parent's side, family life revolved around us. Somehow, we believed we were the two most special people on the planet.

Dad worked hard, while Mom stayed home to raise us in our quiet Midwestern town. Our dog completed the picture-perfect, cookie-cutter family life in early 1980s America. My parents never fought, and Mom kept the house "clean enough to live in but dirty enough to be lived in."

Dad provided security, while Mom exuded serenity.

New BEGINNINGS

I hurried home on the last day of school, my fourth grade report card clutched tightly in my hand. "I can't wait to show Dad how well I've done."

I flung open the door — to a maternal hurricane of flying suds and whirling mops. My mouth dropped open as I watched her dash to the kitchen for a moment and return to the living room, armed with the vacuum in one hand and a dust rag in the other.

I shut my gaping mouth and backed — speechless — into my bedroom. I heard Mom picking objects up to dust and bang them back into their place.

When she charged past my door to rattle around in the bathroom, I tiptoed forth.

"What's going on?" I asked.

Mom slapped the toilet seat down and began scouring the bathroom sink. Dinnertime came, and Mom stalked into the kitchen and started banging pots and pans.

"Time to eat. Go call your sister."

Robin and I sat down, as did Mom. Dad's place remained empty.

"Where's Dad?"

"He's at his mother's house."

"Why?"

"He left."

"He's going to live with Grandmama?"

She began sobbing. "Yes, he wants a divorce." I opened my mouth to ask, "What's that?" but shut it again when Robin shook her head. As the older sister, a graduate of junior high and moving on to senior high in the fall, she liked to look down her nose at her dumber, younger sister.

After a silent dinner, Robin helped Mom clean up, while I retreated to my bedroom. *Whatever is a divorce?* As I pondered the unknowns of the adult world, a brilliant idea hit me. *I'll write Dad a letter and tell him all about my report card.*

After signing it, I tucked it into an envelope and went in search of my mother.

"Can you give me Grandmama's address?"

"Why?" She looked blank.

I held up the letter. "I want to mail this to Dad."

"You won't have to mail it." She began crying again. "I called him and told him he needs to come over and explain things to you kids."

Dad arrived shortly after that.

"Mom says you want a divorce. What's a divorce?"

Dad put his arm around me. "Don't worry your pretty little head, punkin. It just means I need to take a little break. I'm going to stay at Grandmama's for a little while and help her and Grandpa out. You'll still see me. It won't be that bad. I promise. You just pick up the phone if you need anything, and I'll come right over. Deal?"

"Okay, Dad."

This won't be so bad. He just lives a mile away. It'll almost be like always.

"Come here in the kitchen, Caroline," Mom said as soon as she heard Dad's car pull out of our driveway. "Sit on this stool."

New BEGINNINGS

"What're you going to do?"

"It's time for you to be a stylish young lady. I'm going to give you a haircut."

"Dad doesn't like short hair," I said. "He always tells me how much prettier long hair is on girls."

"Look at these pictures." She showed me several girls around my age modeling cute, short haircuts. "Wouldn't you like to look like them?"

"I guess. But Dad doesn't like short hair," I repeated.

"He'll love it. You wait and see."

My hair shrank from waist to earlobes with each harsh snip.

I trusted my mom, so I submitted without complaint.

Afterward, Mom swept up every discarded strand and stuffed it all in a box.

"What are you going to do with it?"

"Mail it to your father." She smiled sweetly.

※ ※ ※

No matter what he'd promised, Dad disappeared like morning dew on a hot August morning, and Mom had to take a full-time job. She embraced Robin's high school high-jinx and let her throw wild parties at our house.

Soon, alcohol flowed freely, and cigarettes dangled from lips that cursed as Mom became the coolest adult in Robin's friends' world. Teens began crashing at our house where freedom and booze reigned.

Close to a dozen kids moved in, dragging sleeping bags

HOUSES, HOME AND HARMONY

and suitcases. The only place I had refuge was my bedroom. I felt so unsafe with these rowdy teens living in the same house that I barricaded myself in my room every night and tried to get some sleep despite the loud music, talking and drunken laughter permeating the air.

One night, Mom pushed past the barricade to awaken me in the middle of the night.

"Look at this," she all but shrieked.

I struggled to focus my sleep-drugged eyes on the newspaper she waved under my nose.

"Your dad went and remarried. Shows how much he cares about you. He's just moved on and forgotten all about us."

She read the two names, derision curling her lip. "I hear Adele is a widow. She probably killed her husband just to get your dad. When she tires of him," she stopped and drew a finger across her throat, "she'll waste him, too."

I lay in stunned silence after Mom withdrew. *Oh, gosh. What do I do now? What if she really does kill Dad?* I stuffed my pillow against my mouth and sobbed.

Robin brought home a male friend, and like so many of the other teens, he began hanging around the house. Soon, he took up permanent residence and slept on the living room floor.

One morning, I saw him leave *Mom's* bedroom.

"What are you doing?" I screamed at Mom. "He's young enough to be your son."

New BEGINNINGS

"This is your father's fault." She shrugged. "He abandoned us, so who is he or you or anyone else to dictate the way I run my life? Cliff makes me laugh, so butt out."

Mom told Robin at the dinner table, "You don't tell your dad about Cliff, and I won't tell him about your partying."

Robin shrugged. "Works for me."

Day after day, I retreated to my bedroom. *Life was so good before Dad left. How could he leave me to rot in this cesspool?*

One evening, I prepared for my nightly shower. First, I barricaded the bathroom door with the hamper. Then I stepped into the tub, rinsed down and began shampooing my hair.

I had just started singing when *blam!*

"I'm in the shower," I cried with eyes squeezed shut against the lather. Total helplessness gripped me.

"I want to see her!" I heard Dad thunder.

Dad?

I heard the curtain pull back a tiny bit. I peeked through the suds.

Dad! He leaned in until we stood nose-to-nose. I looked into his eyes until steam fogged his glasses over. My own eyes began to mist with tears.

"Honey," he cried. "I've been trying to see you for months. Your mom's always got an excuse."

Now it all makes sense. Those sudden trips to the mall

HOUSES, HOME AND HARMONY

or McDonald's. The phone calls she answered in her bedroom. The angry whispers.

"I knew you wouldn't forget me!"

"Never," Dad said. "I filed for visitation rights, but now ..." His fist clenched. "I can't believe what she's putting you through. How long have those kids been living here? Forget the visitation. I'm going to file for custody."

After Dad left, I lay in bed, my mind churning. I remembered all the times I'd asked about him, and Mom would tell me he no longer loved me and he was too busy with his new family to care about me.

Dad filed for custody just as he'd promised. Mom received notice that an investigator would come to inspect our home.

"Get rid of all that dirty laundry," Mom said. "I want every trace of those kids removed. I'll be back soon."

She left and returned with boxes of groceries that she'd "borrowed" from her mother. I helped her stock the refrigerator and cupboards with food to stage the perfect home environment.

"You have to help me," Mom said, when she saw me dragging my feet. "They are not good people. They will take you away from me. Your dad's too busy with his new family to care about you. He's all wrapped up in being an instant grandpa."

I shifted into panic mode, trying to save what little I knew and understood of *home*.

The court date fell just as I entered my freshman year.

New BEGINNINGS

Angry Mom and Quiet Dad sat on opposite sides of the room. I felt split down the middle as I heard both sides argue against the other. When they'd finished lobbing angry accusations at one another, the judge announced, "I want everyone here to clear the courtroom." He looked directly at me and smiled. "Except you, Caroline. I want to talk to you."

As soon as everyone vacated, the judge came down from the bench, shedding his big black robe en route. He grabbed a bag from his desk and came to sit by me.

"Here, honey, you want one?" He extended a bag of Oreos. We munched in silence for a few minutes.

"You love your dad?"

I nodded.

"You love your mom?"

Another nod.

"Are you happy where you're living right now, with your mom?"

Silence.

"Is anybody hurting you?"

Robin's moving on with her life. All Mom has is me. Dad has a whole new family. It will be all my fault if Mom loses me. My eyes filled with tears.

"I don't want to have to decide," I said.

"Why not?" His voice remained calm, gentle.

"I don't want it to be my fault."

"I see." He patted my hand, went back to the bench and donned his robe. He nodded to the bailiff. "You can let them in."

HOUSES, HOME AND HARMONY

"I am now ready to rule …"

Mom stood up. "May I say something?"

"Well, sure." The judge looked a bit puzzled by the interruption. "Go on."

"I would like to relinquish all rights to my daughter on the grounds that I not be forced to pay child support *and* I receive open visitation rights."

"You good with that?" He looked at my dad.

"Yes, Your Honor."

"Fine." The judge smacked his gavel. "I accept those terms. Caroline, you will finish this school term with your mother and then move to your dad's home. Case closed."

☙☙☙

The kids in junior high had treated me like a highly contagious leper. First, divorce was almost unheard of at the time, and word of Mom's wild parties shot through neighborhood gossip lines faster than a prairie fire. Parents instructed their children not to associate with me.

Shortly before my life- and home-changing day in court, a new student came to our school.

"You may take that desk there." Our biology teacher pointed to a desk in the corner.

Hi, I'm Caroline. I scribbled a quick note and folded the paper into a tiny square. The moment our teacher turned his back, I flung it to the stranger's corner. She snagged the note, opened and read it. Then she scribbled something and flung it back.

New BEGINNINGS

Hi. Happy to meet you. I'm Connie.

Connie, the new girl in school, and I, ostracized for my mom's parties, became instant friends. Then summer interrupted our friendship. Three months crawled by as I waited to go back to school — high school this time.

I parked myself by the buses and watched the giggling girls and swaggering guys hop off. *Is she here? Did she move away?* Hope waned as each emptied bus moved off.

"Hi!" I turned around. Connie grinned, then hugged me hard. "I'm so happy to see you. I missed you so much!"

Tears sprang up from my lonely, sad soul and spilled over.

I have a real friend. A forever friend. She came to find me — me, whom nobody else wants to be around.

❧❧❧

"You need some meat on your bones," Dad said after I'd moved in with him and Adele. "Didn't your mother feed you?"

Well, as a matter of fact, no.

Preoccupied with nursing bitterness and drowning life in booze, Mom often neglected to feed me. The resident teens bought and labeled their own caches and constantly warned me against raiding their food supplies. After I went from thin to skinny, Mom finally noticed.

"You need to eat." She set food in front of me. *You need to eat. You need to do the laundry. Don't touch my food. Keep out of my room.*

HOUSES, HOME AND HARMONY

Weary of orders from all sides and feeling powerless and invisible in my own home, I discovered one lonely, sole power. I could *and would* refuse to eat.

"You need to eat that," Mom repeated, irritation tinting her voice.

No, I don't. And you can't make me.

But now, at Dad's, the fridge, cupboards and pantry all overflowed with food. Beautiful, tasty, yummy food.

Adele cooked a spaghetti dinner, complete with salad and dessert.

"This is so good," I said, savoring every bite. "Thank you, Adele."

She beamed and passed me another roll.

"Good to see you eating," Dad remarked. "You'll be at a healthy weight in no time."

Unaccustomed to so much, I quickly became nauseous and dashed to the bathroom. Moments later, my churning stomach emptied itself into the toilet.

Whew. I feel so much better, I thought, wiping my mouth and rinsing it out.

I ate everything in sight as Dad and Adele encouraged me on.

"I'm getting fat," I said as my weight increased.

"No, you're not," Dad said. "Now you are at a healthy weight. You're beautiful."

I'm not beautiful. I'm fat. Kids love to tease fat kids. I scowled at my reflection in the mirror. Then I remembered my first taste of Adele's cooking — that delicious spaghetti dinner. I remembered gorging until I

New BEGINNINGS

thought I would pop. I remembered how *good* I felt after I vomited.

I went into the bathroom, gagged myself with my toothbrush. Soon, my dinner swirled around in the toilet bowl. I smiled to myself. *I think I just found the solution to having so much good food under my nose, keeping Dad happy and keeping myself thin.*

❦❦❦

"Would you like to go to church with my family on Sunday?" Connie asked as we parted for the weekend.

"Sure. I've not been to church much. My grandpa used to take me to his church sometimes." *Besides, a little God in my life might help it make some sense.* The first thing I noticed was a drum set, a keyboardist and several guitarists on stage. *No organ? This should be cool!*

The music began with a thud, and soon the walls vibrated from ramped-up amps. I threw myself into the service, clapping and singing like everybody else.

Suddenly, an elderly lady appeared in the aisle next to my seat. As the music throbbed on, the pastor and his wife came down off the platform and began yelling at the lady in a language I'd never heard.

The lady passed out. Somebody covered her inert body with a sheet, and the music pulsed on.

I screamed and fled to the parking lot. "Help, help!" I screamed. "There's a dead lady in there, and nobody seems to *care*. Somebody call an ambulance — quick!"

HOUSES, HOME AND HARMONY

Connie's family followed, hot on my heels.

"Caroline, Caroline, calm down." Connie's mom, Annie, put her arm around me. "Come on, Arnold, let's take Caroline home."

I climbed in the backseat, shaking, while the family piled in after me and giggled.

"Don't worry," Arnold said, grinning at me through the rearview mirror. "You're just not used to the way we Pentecostals worship."

"Maybe we should have warned you," Annie agreed, "especially if you've had little experience in church."

"Grandpa's church sure was different. We kids were pretty much just told to be quiet and behave."

I stared out the window as the family chattered on. *I can't believe they're willing to miss out on church just because of me.*

"I'm sorry for being so stupid," I said.

"You're not stupid." Annie turned around to squeeze my hand. "The pastor simply prayed for the lady to receive the Holy Spirit. It must've looked scary to you, but trust us, it's a good thing."

Whatever that means. I kept my mouth shut but basked in the love and acceptance that filled the car.

Connie's family bought me coloring books with Bible stories in them. Stories I'd never heard in my life — God keeping hungry lions from eating a guy named Daniel? Three men surviving in a furnace, while their captors died just for tossing them in? A dude named Jonah surviving three days inside a whale?

New BEGINNINGS

As I colored, along with Connie's younger siblings, her parents told me story after story of God's goodness and provision and love.

"You're right. Your church scared me because I'm not used to it. I want to go back and try it again." I laughed. "I promise not to run out screaming again."

"You can do whatever you want in our church. Jump if you want to jump. Shout if you want to shout. God likes his people to interact with him. Think about a football game. We go nuts, cheering for our favorite teams. Why shouldn't we go nuts while praising — that means cheering — God?"

❧ ❧ ❧

Mom used to send me to stay at Grandma's house while she worked. The kids on her block hung out together, and now that I lived at Dad's, I had the freedom to do the same. That's how I met Franky.

Franky was everything my family wasn't. A complete free spirit. I followed rules and tried to please everyone in my life. Franky broke rules and tried to please no one but himself. I loved hanging around with him and absorbing his carefree attitude and outlook on life. He was a lot of fun and made me laugh — a rare commodity in my life.

That first taste of independence made me heady. After a while, Franky and I hung out alone.

I love being around Franky. He helps me relax, I thought, jumping in his car. We dashed off to a major city, an hour away, without a second thought.

HOUSES, HOME AND HARMONY

We drifted from hanging with friends to hanging together to having casual, unplanned, uncommitted sex. No problem. No worries.

"Hey, Caroline, could you babysit for me today?" Adele's daughter Allison asked over the phone. "I need to get some Christmas shopping done."

"Sure. What time?"

"Come for dinner. I'll leave after that."

I went over to Allison's, and as soon as I walked into her kitchen, my stomach reeled. I immediately vomited on her floor.

"Caroline, are you okay?" Allison ran over and put an arm around me. "I hope you don't have the flu. I don't want my kids sick over the holidays."

"I'm fine. No big deal." I swaggered just like Franky would. "Must be whatever you're cooking."

"Maybe you're pregnant." Allison giggled.

"Well, maybe I am." I deepened my swagger.

"Caroline, that was a joke." Allison peered into my face. "Are you and Franky sexually active?"

"Yeah. What of it?"

When Allison returned from her shopping, she handed me a box. "You have to pee on that stick," she said, grinning.

"You're being ridiculous. I'm not pregnant." I laughed with her.

"Whatever. Just pee on the stick."

New BEGINNINGS

I did as she asked and handed the stick back. "See, I'm okay."

Allison looked at it and then up at me. "Caroline," she said, "this is serious. You *are* pregnant."

What? I choked on my jokes. *This can't be real. It can't.*

Allison left the bathroom. After a few minutes, I followed and found her sitting, stunned, in the kitchen.

"I called my mom."

"Why did you do that?"

"This isn't a joke, Caroline. You're going to have to tell your dad."

Adele came over, in tears.

For the first time the reality of it all hit me in the pit of my stomach.

How can I break this news to Dad? He's worked so hard to keep me from the awful life I had before, and this is how I repay him?

"I'm going to go to Connie's," I said, bolting for the door. *I need to get away and think.*

I pounded on their door a short time later.

Arnold opened the door. I burst into tears.

"I have to talk to Connie," I said. "Right away."

"I'm sorry, she's not home, but come in, come in."

"You're always welcome here." Annie had come to the door when she heard my hysterical sobbing. "What's wrong, Caroline? You know you can tell us."

"I will if you promise not to tell Connie. I want to tell her myself."

HOUSES, HOME AND HARMONY

"Of course, dear, of course." Annie put an arm around me and gave me a gentle squeeze.

"I'm pregnant. I know God's punishing me for screwing up. Dad's going to be so disappointed. He'll throw me out and make me go back to Mom's. And she's going to throw it in his face and tell him what a lousy parent he is." My sobbing intensified as all my fears bubbled from my lips.

"Caroline, Caroline, calm down." Annie wrapped me in a full embrace. "A baby's not punishment from God. A baby is a *gift*! I don't think your dad will throw you out, but if he does, you are welcome to come and live here with us. Please understand how much we love you!"

Next, I went to see Franky. "I need to tell you something."

"Okay. What's up?"

I pulled the test stick out of my pocket and handed it to him.

"See this?"

"Yeah, what of it?"

"It says I'm pregnant."

"Oh." He shrugged. "That's cool."

I went home, and dinner proceeded normally. *At least Adele isn't crying.* I ate quickly and got up.

"Stay," Dad said. "You haven't had dessert yet." He got up and went to the refrigerator. *I need to get outta here.*

I gobbled it down. "Now can I go?"

"Don't you have something you want to tell me?"

New BEGINNINGS

"No, not really."

I saw a tear slip down Adele's cheek. *She's told him.*

"Are you sure there's not something you want to talk about?"

"No, what would we need to be talking about?"

"How about talking about what you don't want to talk about."

Yep, she told him. He already knows.

I stared down at my dirty dishes.

"I'm pregnant."

"You need to get an abortion."

"No." *Did I just say no to Dad?* "We'll take care of the baby."

"So, where's Franky now?"

"We're in it together. He said he'll get a job. I don't want an abortion."

The phone rang. Dad picked up the receiver and dropped it back to disconnect. It rang again. He repeated the action. It rang again. Dad unplugged the phone and came back to the table.

"Honey, I just don't want you to be saddled with so much responsibility so young. You're too young to have a baby. So you made a wrong choice. That's okay. But you need to be established to take care of a baby. You're not an adult, you're still a baby yourself."

I knew Dad was trying to reason with me and set out the facts in methodical fashion. But I kept thinking how disappointed he was in me. How badly I failed him. He worked so hard, and I let myself get knocked up.

HOUSES, HOME AND HARMONY

A baby is a gift from God. I remembered Arnold's and Annie's words.

"We'll do what we have to do," I said to Dad, "but I don't want an abortion."

"It looks like you've already made up your mind." I saw the hurt in Dad's eyes as he plugged the phone back in. It was ringing.

"Hello. Hold on, Connie." He handed the receiver to me. "It's for you."

"What's going on?" she cried. "Mom said it's important, but she wouldn't tell me. I've been trying to call for the last hour."

"I'm pregnant. What am I going to do?"

"Um … you're going to have a baby, Caroline. That's how it works."

ঽ৽ঽ৽ঽ৽

Franky and I moved into our apartment the week I graduated high school, very thin and six months pregnant. He got a job to support me and our coming child.

I settled into my new home determined to make everything cookie-cutter perfect.

This is my own little dinette set. My own little couch. Nobody can take it away from me.

I threw up five and six times every day of my pregnancy, this time from sickness and not from purging. But I kept it secret because I didn't want anyone to know about the bulimia. Only Connie knew, and she could be trusted with a secret.

New BEGINNINGS

I had a doctor's appointment on my baby's due date.

"Hello, Caroline. I'm Dr. Smith. Dr. Jones is at the hospital delivering another baby at this very moment, so I'll take care of you today. I'm happy to meet you."

She glanced at my chart and then me. "So, how far along are you?"

"I, um, actually, I'm due today."

"You look pretty small."

"Oh, it's nothing. I've been a little nauseous, morning pukes, nothing big."

She studied the chart again. "You've *lost* 30 pounds since your first visit. Pregnant ladies are supposed to *gain* weight, not *lose*. I'm sending you for an ultrasound right now and see what's going on."

The tech remained silent throughout the procedure. Finally she flicked on the light and said, "Go ahead and get dressed. I'm giving this to the doctor. You'll need to see her."

I dressed and returned to the little waiting room.

Dr. Smith came in.

"I'm sorry, Caroline, but you need to go to the hospital right now."

"Why?"

"Your baby is in danger. He needs to be delivered — today."

"Oh, okay. Thanks." *I'm going to have my baby today,* my heart sang. I never processed the words "your baby is in danger." I called my mom and Connie as soon as I settled in at the hospital. "I'm having my baby today."

HOUSES, HOME AND HARMONY

Mom showed up.
Connie and her parents arrived.
Dad came with Adele.
Franky sauntered in with his mom and grandmother.

Soon anger and accusations flew. While Connie's family prayed in one corner, mine squared off in another.

"If you hadn't left home, Caroline wouldn't be in this mess."

"Of course, your home was a haven of tranquility with all those delinquents hanging around."

Monitor alarms went off. A nurse rushed in. "Your baby's heart stopped." She rolled me this way and that, trying to stimulate it into pumping again.

"I'm sorry, but you'll have to remove your jewelry."

I took off the necklace Franky had given me and handed it to Mom. She nervously tangled and untangled it in her hands.

"Stop that," Franky barked. "You're going to break it."

"Yeah, like you broke my daughter's life. You knocked her up!" Dad yelled.

Finally, the nurse got me in the position like downward dog in yoga, my butt in the air, head down, and there I stayed for the next agonizing hours. When I puked, I wiped my mouth on the hospital sheet. Nobody noticed.

Can't they all just go away?

"We can't wait for natural delivery." Dr. Smith clipped her words as she strode into the room.

"It's about time." Adele stood her full 4 foot, 10 inches. "This girl's been suffering long enough."

New BEGINNINGS

"I agree. We're taking her down to OR for a C-section right now."

The orderlies wheeled me away from the cacophony. *Peace at last.*

The doctor's words, "Your baby is in danger," had yet to settle.

I awakened in my quiet, empty hospital room and pressed the nurses' button.

"Where is everybody?" I asked.

"Home, I imagine. You've been out for two days."

"Two days?" I ached everywhere and felt physically empty.

"My baby's born?"

"Yes."

"Do I have a boy or a girl?"

"You have a son. The pediatrician will be in soon to talk to you."

Dad showed up first, followed by Franky and his mother. My stomach retched at the cheeseburger she offered.

The pediatrician tapped on my door and stepped in.

"I'm going to get right to it," she said. "We can't keep anything in your baby's stomach. He isn't able to maintain his body temperature. He's probably not going to survive." She paused. "The next 24 hours are crucial."

Two days later and still baffled at my son's undiagnosed condition, the doctor had him transported to the nearest children's hospital, an hour away.

HOUSES, HOME AND HARMONY

We lived the next four months in "the next 24 hours are crucial" mode, while doctors tested, discussed, retested and failed to find a diagnosis.

I drove to the hospital every day, while Franky lived life.

"I'm sorry, Caroline, but there's nothing else we can do. We're going to let you take your son home to die. We've already contacted Comfort Care, which is home hospice for babies."

I drove Ian home. Twelve hours later, I had to dial 911.

"My baby's turning blue."

The EMT seemed in amble mode as he drove us back to the hospital where Ian was born. *He probably expects him to die, too, so why rush?*

The trauma doctor sent Ian back to Children's Hospital where we spent the next two months.

"There's one test we haven't done," Dr. Johnson said. "Your son shows all the markers of this particular disorder. It's rare. Very rare."

Hot diggity dog! Finally we'll have some answers, and the doctors can fix Ian.

"I wish I had better news," Dr. Johnson said after the tests were completed, "but my hunch was right. Ian has septo-optic dysplasia."

"What is that?"

Dr. Johnson drew a thick medical dictionary from under his arm and began flipping through the pages. He stopped, turned the book toward me and pointed.

New BEGINNINGS

Under the syndrome listing I read, "Fluke of nature."

I looked at Dr. Johnson. "What does that mean?"

"It means we have no idea. Your son's chances of survival are very slim. He'll probably be blind and will require intensive care to survive."

He can't be fixed. The reality of my son's condition finally sank into my young brain. I took Ian home along with mountains of instructions.

We lived 24 hours at a time.

❧❧❧

"I need some help," I told Franky one evening. "I'm so tired. I need a nap."

"You wanted the kid," he said. "He's all yours. You deal with it."

Every night I wondered if I'd find my son dead in the morning. Every day I feared it could be his last.

The hours alone made it feel like nobody came to see me or my doomed son.

One day Connie showed up at my door. "Give me that baby," she said, tossing her handbag on the couch and stretching out both hands.

"Don't you need a bath or something?" she asked, snuggling her nose against Ian's. "Go take a soak. We'll be fine."

Later, as I dressed in my room, I heard Connie singing to Ian, as though he were a normal, thriving baby. Tears pricked behind my eyelids.

He's important. He has value. He's my gift from God.

HOUSES, HOME AND HARMONY

"I can't be!" I cried when Ian was about 8 months old.

I had awakened nauseous and dashed for the toilet.

"Can't be what?" Franky asked, padding into the bathroom and yawning.

"Pregnant. But I can't be. I'm on birth control."

"You've got to be kidding," he barked. "How could you be so stupid?"

How am I going to manage with another baby when Ian is already so sick? Shame enveloped me.

"Mom, I can't take it," I wailed over the phone. "I can't even wrap my head around another baby with Ian's care keeping me tied down 24/7. It's going to be impossible."

"You sit tight, I'm coming right over."

Mom arrived and took charge. She looked at me, disheveled and slightly smelly, and the house that looked like a prairie tornado had passed through.

"Get yourself cleaned up and dressed. We're going out."

"Where?"

"You'll see." She reached for Ian. "Just let me snuggle with my grandson until you pull yourself together."

I scrambled to obey, and soon Mom had us packed up in her car. She drove all the way back to Children's Hospital and ushered me, holding Ian in my arms, into the lobby.

"Sit down, Caroline, and look around. What do you see?"

"What do you mean?"

New BEGINNINGS

"Take a real good look." Mom flung out an arm. "Do you see them — all the parents and families coming in and out of this place? Their children are here, some so sick they will never leave. You could still be here, but you're not. You have been given the opportunity to give Ian a normal life. Take advantage of what is right in front of you. Stop waiting for him to die and just live."

I stood up, holding my living baby tightly. "Thanks, Mom." Tears filled my eyes. I knew she was right. "We can go home now. Ian and I are ready to *live*."

Franky and I stayed together, but he pretty much checked out after Daisy's birth.

He worked two jobs and spent the rest of the time with his unattached, unencumbered friends.

I felt suffocated and unappreciated, while the dream of perfect home and family faded into despair.

"I need to get a job," I told my doctor, when Ian was around 2 1/2 and Daisy about 14 months old.

"I think that's entirely feasible." She smiled. "Ian has done remarkably well under your care. He's fortunate to have such a good mommy." She jiggled Ian's foot, and he giggled. "I think you can safely leave him with a sitter now."

Connie and I both got jobs at a local factory, working the nightshift.

A neighbor watched the children three hours every morning so I could snatch a little sleep.

All week I planned what I would do with my very first

paycheck. I bought clothes for the kids and paint to spruce up their bedroom.

"Look at this," I babbled to Franky, when he came home from work. I held up the paint can. "Isn't this a cute color?"

"Where's my part?"

"Your part of what?"

"I want *my* part of the money, stupid."

"I used my check to get these things for the kids."

"All of it?"

"Yes. Why not?"

"I want part of your check."

"You're kidding me!" I screamed. "You already work two jobs. What do you need more money for?"

"I wish that kid had never been born."

"That kid is your son, Franky."

"Don't care. Wish you'd just die and get out of my life, too."

"I can't take it any longer," I cried to Connie the next night at work. "I need to get out, but how? Where could I go?"

"How about that low-income housing in the next county?"

Living on my own empowered me. I felt sure I could hold down a real job and still be a good mother to my children.

However, the pace wore me down. When my parents tried to help, I copped an attitude. *You weren't there when*

New BEGINNINGS

I needed you, so don't go poking your noses in my business now.

❧❧❧

"Hey, Caroline." My co-worker approached my bench at work. "Would you go out with me tonight? I'm meeting my boyfriend at Jake's Bar and don't want to go alone."

"I'm not much of a drinker, and I've never been in a bar."

"That's okay. Just come and be with me, okay? I'd feel safer with you there."

"Well, all right."

"Can you go with me again tonight?" Carrie asked.

"Not to the same bar," I said. "That bartender was so rude."

"Well, how about the one next door?"

"Fine."

We walked in. The rude bartender sat across from Carrie's boyfriend. I scowled down at both guys.

"Brothers," Rude Bartender said, pointing to the other guy and then himself. "I'm sorry I treated you so shoddy last night. No excuses. Forgive me? I'm Truman."

After that night, no matter where Carrie met her boyfriend, Truman would be there. We began talking and then dating on our own. I sensed strength in him, a stability I'd been longing for all my life. I'd had fun with Franky when we first met. Two children later and living alone, fun no longer attracted me. With Truman, I felt safe.

HOUSES, HOME AND HARMONY

A few months later, I got really sick at work and asked Connie to drop me off at Truman's house. We arrived at 6 a.m.

"I'm sorry to barge in on you," I said, "but I'm so sick. Can I crash here for a little while? The kids are at the sitter's."

"Sure. I don't have to go to work until late afternoon."

I struggled to open my eyes when I felt someone shaking me.

"Caroline, wake up." Truman bent over me. "You are burning up with fever, and I have to leave for work soon. You want me to call your mom?"

"No, just take me home. I have to get the kids."

I collected my kids and went home. Once there, I kept passing in and out of consciousness, and my eyelids felt like iron weights hung from them.

I awakened around 11 p.m. and dashed to the toilet to puke. Blood swirled around in the bowl. My head pounded and felt so heavy I had to cradle it in the crook of my elbow. I crawled downstairs and tried to call Truman. The phone rang and rang. *I'll bet he can't hear the phone ringing over the loud music at the bar.*

I called Mom.

"I'll be right over." As she helped me dress, she pulled my pants up to my waist and let go. They fell straight to the floor.

"What have you done to yourself?"

Shame pushed through the nausea and my pounding head. *This is all my fault. I tried to quit binging and*

New BEGINNINGS

purging, I really did. It's all just too much. Too much.

Mom drove me to the emergency room. I weighed in at 89 pounds. The doctor immediately had me whisked to the ICU.

I awakened five days later. I turned my head and saw Truman hunched over in a chair by the bed, napping.

"Truman?"

He roused immediately.

"You awake?" I heard the relief in his voice. "I've been here every minute possible."

Later, the nurse came in and informed me I'd be transferred to a regular room.

"Your doctor will talk to you after the move."

"We need to address your problem," the doctor said the moment he came into the room.

"What problem?"

"The constant vomiting."

"Oh, that." I shrugged. "I'm just ..."

"Caroline." He parked in the chair and crossed his arms. "We know what you've been doing. We know you've been binging and purging and what it's done to your body. And now, here's what we're going to do about it."

Busted. My deepest, darkest secret lay open between us.

"You are going to stay in the hospital until you gain 25 pounds, and you will be monitored. Believe me, we will know if you cheat."

HOUSES, HOME AND HARMONY

A nurse sat and watched me eat every bite of food from every plate. I was forbidden to use the toilet for an hour after each meal and snack.

"I will never go through this again," Truman said. He had been to visit every day as I crawled toward my target weight. He stared into my eyes, pain and anger mirrored on his face.

"Go through what?"

"I will not stay and watch you self-destruct again."

"What?"

"You have so much to live for." He stood up and paced the room like a trapped animal. "Beautiful kids. Connie. Your parents. A good job. You've worked so hard to get where you are. Why would you throw it all away?"

I kept my eyes glued to my fingers picking at the sheet.

"Why on earth are you trying to destroy yourself?"

I stared out the window. Puffy white clouds drifted past.

"Tell me why."

"Because …" I focused on the *drip, drip, drip* of the IV. "Because it feels better to hurt myself than let anybody else hurt me. I can control hurting myself. I can't control others hurting me."

"Look at me, Caroline." His tone turned hard, yet gentle. "I will *never* hurt you. I will protect you. You don't have to do this to yourself any longer."

൙൙൙

New BEGINNINGS

Soon after my release, I was forced to move again. Connie and Truman helped me.

"Why don't you stay for dinner?" I asked after Connie left. "You've been so helpful, the least I can do is cook a decent meal for you."

"Sounds like an offer I can't refuse." Truman grinned.

He stayed for dinner. He never left.

The following June, the kids and I wanted to do something special for Truman, who was their father in every sense except blood. I let them stay up until he got home from work, and we hid in the dark until he flipped on the living room light.

"Surprise!" we cried, jumping from our hiding places. "Happy Father's Day. We're going to celebrate *you*!"

The kids gave him their homemade Father's Day cards. I gave him a collage of photos of him with the kids. We ate cupcakes, and then I tucked the kids in for the night.

"You can't one-up me," Truman said when I returned to the dining room.

"What?"

"You just gave me the best gift ever," he explained, "but I can top it."

"Huh?"

He left and returned a few minutes later with a tiny box.

"I love you. I love your kids." He opened the box. "Will you let me be their forever dad?"

HOUSES, HOME AND HARMONY

I clutched the box to my chest. Tears blurred the ring nestled in its black velvet cushion. *Can this really be happening?*

"Yes, yes!" I threw myself into his arms.

We married three months later. Not a sliver of doubt clouded the day. *I am marrying my friend and protector.*

❧❧❧

"Caroline, would you come with me to see our church's Christmas play?" Connie asked a year after Truman and I married.

"Sure, I'll come." The play moved me enough to accept that God desires relationship with all his creation — yes, even with *me* — so I began attending Trinity Full Gospel every Sunday. I took Ian and Daisy for Sunday school and left our newest bundled blessing, whom we named Macy, at home with her doting daddy, Truman.

About six months later, the pastor asked if he could stop by for a visit.

"What a beautiful set," he said, referring to my 100-year-old dining table and chairs.

"Thank you. I love this set."

"Have you ever wondered what stories antiques have to tell? How many of life's decisions were made by someone sitting on these very chairs?"

"I never thought about it before. I'll be looking at this set with new eyes from now on."

The next Sunday, he got up to preach. "Have you ever

New BEGINNINGS

wondered as you pass by the houses in your neighborhood — nice ones and rundown ones — who lives in them? What is their history? What events have those houses witnessed of the people inhabiting them? What goes on in people's minds? Can we see their strengths or weaknesses, joys or sorrows, just by looking at them?"

He's talking to me, I thought as I sat and hung on every word. *I'm so weighed down by life, and I'm tired of carrying it all.*

"If anyone here would like to give his or her burdens and failures and fears to God right now, just come up here to the front. I want to pray with you."

I jumped up and immediately felt like a pile of rocks, stones of worry and sorrow and regret lay piled at my feet. I floated to the front. A sense of the peace of God enveloped me as Pastor Terry came to pray with me.

God, you are the security I've been looking for all my life. I felt so unsafe under Mom's roof with all those teens bunking at our house. I felt like a big fat failure at Dad's. I know I disappointed him so much when I let myself get knocked up. And those years with Franky, I felt so completely alone, like I was at the bottom of a deep well and up to my neck in water. Nobody cared. Nobody helped.

Then you put Truman in my life. He became my safety net on a human level. He has loved me, cherished me and always made me feel safe. But I needed more. I needed a Savior to save me from myself, even more than what Truman could do. I needed someone who could take all my failures and shortcomings away and make me new and clean. Truman can't do all that for me. Only Jesus can do that because only Jesus is God.

All my life, I've struggled to please everybody, but Pastor Terry says you love me just as I am. Fat or skinny. Despite my bad choices. Failures. Struggles. Nothing affects your love for me. For the first time in my life, I feel completely loved, accepted and clean. From now on, I am yielding my whole life, soul and body to you, God, because only you can fix me.

"I did the most amazing thing today at church," I told Truman when I got home that day.

"What?"

"I gave my heart to God." I twirled — *twirled* — around the room and flung my hands wide. "I feel so light!"

Truman began attending Trinity Full Gospel after that. Eventually, he gave his heart to God, too.

॰॰॰

My heart swells with love and gratitude as I watch my "perfect" son, Ian, who has never hidden behind a "handicap." We always say he's "handy-capable." He throws himself into every activity open to other kids, despite the condition we've since learned to be De Morsier syndrome. He has worked in an attorney general's office and graduated high school. We all cheer him on as he anticipates college.

New BEGINNINGS

God has used my son to show me how to live. Ian trusts his hearing to compensate for what he can't see. Likewise, I can't see God, but I can hear him through praying to him, worshiping him and reading his words in the Bible.

I smile when I sit in church and see Truman resting his strong, gentle arm across Daisy's shoulders. I believe God has adopted us into his family, just as Truman adopted Ian and Daisy and loves them as he does Macy, the daughter God gave us the year after we married. I realized that God's given me the home I'd longed for from the day Dad left. I even have two families now. There is the one I share with Truman and our three children. The other, Trinity Full Gospel, is where I'm still free to jump when I want to jump and praise God with all my being.

THE ONE
The Story of Bella
Written by Melissa Harding

The sound of my father's hand against my mother's cheek echoed down the hall as I huddled against my sister, wishing I could disappear into the paper-thin walls. We crouched in the corner of our room, hiding behind the bed from the screams that filled our home.

"It's okay, sissy." My sister Abby whispered in my ear, trying to steady my trembling body with her arm.

My heart raced against the ticking of the clock as I fought to breathe. Like a fish out of water, I gulped for air, but my chest squeezed tight against my efforts. As if an elephant sat unmoving on my chest, I wriggled against its weight. Another asthma attack would only make things worse.

"Bella, it's okay," Abby said again. "They're done. We can go out now."

My heart slowed at her words, and I took a deep breath, letting the air fill the emptiness in my lungs. But my fear never left. It wormed its way so deep into my being, I could never escape. There was one thing I could count on in our home: mayhem.

Maybe it's because of me, I wondered. Like a steel anchor, guilt pinned me down, convincing me of my worthlessness.

New BEGINNINGS

❧❧❧

I was born on a crisp fall day in Orville, Ohio. With the umbilical cord wrapped around my neck, I entered this world short of breath and short of hope. My early years passed by with a constant barrage of violence and chaos. My daddy was a bootlegger and my mommy, a devout Christian. I learned quickly how to behave based on my surroundings and circumstances. If Daddy came home after drinking beer, he was sweet and gentle. If he came home after drinking whiskey, though, we knew to expect something different. On the ride home from kindergarten, I often leaned my head against the window of the bus, knowing the bumpy ride would give me a headache. Daddy and Mommy wouldn't fight if I was sick. They always took care of me, so I tried my best to make our home happy by making myself sick. Mommy wanted to do "the right thing" and stay married. She was a brave, unwavering woman who stood firm on what she believed in. She never shrank back from letting Daddy know what she thought about his ungodly ways.

"Doug, I'm tired of the alcohol. You know how much I hate it." Mom begged for the thousandth time, her voice rising as it quavered with both anger and fear. There was nowhere to hide in the car, so Abby and I braced ourselves for the coming storm.

"Carol, how many times do I have to tell you to shut up about it?" He reached over and slapped her across the face, leaving a bright red imprint of his fingers across her cheek.

THE ONE

My mom and grandma took my sister and me to church, so I grew up hearing stories about God answering prayers. My prayers grew stronger as the storm in our home raged fiercely around me.

"God," I begged. "Make it stop! I'll go ahead and die if Daddy will give his life to Jesus and stop hitting Mommy! Please, just make it stop."

My prayers fell flat as another smack jolted me back to reality.

What's wrong with our family? I asked myself again and again, trying to keep the tears from escaping. I loved my mom and dad. They weren't the problem. It was me. It must be me. There must be something wrong with me.

My little voice rose over the yelling, and I began to sing along to the music playing in our cassette player. A hush fell over the car, and the yelling faded as music filled the air. They always stopped fighting when I started singing. Besides getting sick, it was one thing I could do that made them forget their anger.

☙☙☙

"Girls, your daddy is dead."

My mom's words reached my ears, but my 7-year-old mind couldn't understand their meaning. Panic rose, and the elephant returned to take its place upon my chest. I heaved under its weight, grasping for air — grasping for an escape from the suffocating truth. The air felt like a thick milkshake sucked through a thin straw. I couldn't get enough, no matter how hard I sucked it in.

New BEGINNINGS

When I was 5, we had moved to Kentucky to be closer to my dad's family. Daddy worked as a truck driver for an oil company. The mountain roads were dangerous on the best of days. But that day, sheets of rain had dumped from the sky, making the winding road a river of fury. My mom explained how Daddy had jumped from the cab, but the tanker truck carrying 7,800 gallons of crude oil careened out of control, and somehow he was pinned underneath it.

Abby bolted out of the house and up the road, but her screams drifted back into the room, piercing the air with their agony. Daddy was gone. He left me. I tried to understand, but like a puzzle that's missing too many pieces, nothing made sense. The familiar feeling of guilt slithered up my spine, and terror gripped my mind.

"No! He can't be dead!" I cried, my lungs wheezing and my heart racing. Fear clawed its way through my veins, and I fought against the truth as my lungs fought for air.

God, I prayed for you to stop it, but not this way!

"Bella, breathe!" My mom held me, and I clung to her, gasping for both air and hope, but my little body couldn't find either.

Had God twisted my prayer? Maybe it was my fault. Somehow or someway, I could've done something different. I could've been better or done something more.

We moved back to Ohio, but I couldn't shake the feeling of abandonment and rejection I felt from both my dad and from God.

THE ONE

❧❧❧

Brandon slipped into my life with the promise of fun and excitement. I was 12 years old, but my body looked more mature. The day Brandon waltzed up to my sister's car, I melted into his attention and affection. Although he was much older, I reveled in his interest. The little girl inside me wanted desperately to be loved, and I had learned to act in ways I thought people wanted me to act. I did the things Brandon asked me to do. I didn't want to displease anyone, and so I traded my innocence for the illusion of love and acceptance.

My mom and grandma continued taking me to church, and I loved everything about it. During one service, I went forward, got baptized and committed my life to following God. In my head, I believed that God was real and Jesus was loving. But it never made it into my heart. I only knew him on the surface, and I had no idea who I was other than an abandoned, worthless girl. Without an identity or an anchor, I ran from person to person, hoping I would eventually find someone to fill the aching void within me. An insatiable hunger to be loved permeated my heart, but the voices that hounded my mind told me I wouldn't ever be good enough. Their words crept into every part of my being until, finally, I conceded to what I thought was the truth. I could play the part, but I would never be worthy of a love that would last forever.

As the years went by, I went along with whatever

New BEGINNINGS

anyone around me was doing. When my friends started drinking and taking drugs, I got swept up in a current that both thrilled and terrified me. The bar became a haven, the place I came alive. Before long, I realized how free alcohol made me feel. When I was drunk, I didn't have to be the shy, scared little girl I kept hidden inside. I became the person I wanted to be — free.

After Brandon came a series of older men. I went to Planned Parenthood and starting taking birth control. It only took one time of forgetting to take the pill and my whole world turned upside down.

"You're pregnant, aren't you?" My mom's suspicions rose as my behavior changed.

"Yeah." I said, unable to deal with the gnawing fear.

"We'll figure this out, okay?" Her words gave me hope, but the road would be anything but straight or easy.

My mom taught me the basics of being a mother, and my little girl arrived healthy and beautiful. I loved my sweet baby, but the stress of being a high school mom overwhelmed me. I couldn't escape the emptiness I felt inside. The unquenchable longing to find someone who loved me drew me again and again to the next relationship. I was desperate for someone who would fill the void in my heart. The only place I knew to look was to men. Feeling their arms around me, no matter how temporary it was, made me feel worth something. By the time I was 19, another baby from another man entered the world.

THE ONE

☙☙☙

I ran the knife over my wrist, thinking about how it would feel when the blade sliced through my skin. It would be so easy, and then all the pain would go away.

Again the thoughts plagued me, following me throughout my days, chasing me into the night. *Look at all your mistakes. You're so stupid. Two babies with two different men. No one is ever going to love you. You're worthless.* Like the perpetual leak of a faucet, the thoughts dripped incessantly. I daydreamed about the different ways I could kill myself. I would take pills and every day add another one.

My kids would be better off without me, I concluded. *They don't need me and all my stupid mistakes.* When I messed up as a mom, the feelings of guilt magnified until all I could see when I looked in the mirror was a heaping pile of regret.

I slammed on the brakes, dirt billowing around the car, my knuckles white from gripping the steering wheel. I had driven to the edge of a cliff, planning to drive off and end my misery, but I stopped at the last second. As much as I dreamed of ending my life, I never could go through with it. *I'll go to hell if I kill myself.* Words from another lifetime broke through the haze of my depression, reminding me of my days in church and the fear of an eternity in torment.

"No one stays!" I screamed. First Daddy, and now every man I'd ever given myself to. I often found comfort

New BEGINNINGS

in the arms of different men. The temporary illusion of love was better than the loneliness that threatened to eat me alive. At least the guys at the bar wanted me, even if it was only in the shadows of night. They always fled with the rising sun. I didn't expect anything more, though. With all my mistakes, I didn't deserve any better. I was unworthy of love, especially God's love. I had thought about going back to church, but I was too ashamed to stand before God. Why would he want anything to do with me when I had made so many stupid mistakes? The main reason I didn't want to kill myself was because I was pretty sure God would send me to hell if I did, but most of the time it was all I thought about. I felt unworthy of anything good in life.

By the time I was 21, I'd given birth to a third child by yet another man. I was alone with three babies to raise. But my fear of rejection only furthered my desire to find true love. If I just kept looking, I would find the perfect man who wouldn't ever leave. Perhaps just around the corner, Prince Charming was waiting to swoop in and rescue me. Lots of men had swooped in, that was for sure, but once they had their fill, they wrung me out like an old rag. I wasn't worthy enough to be choosy, though, and I picked men who wouldn't reject my overtures. Not surprisingly, these men were often found under the neon lights of a bar. In the haze of an intoxicated delirium, I traded my body for the fleeting mirage of fulfillment.

Maybe someday I would find my happy ending.

THE ONE

❧❧❧

A knock at the door jolted me awake, and I stumbled to the door, wiping the sleep from my eyes. I looked through the peephole, and my heart skipped a beat. It was Dillon, the guy I brought home from the bar the week before.

He wants to see me, I thought, joy surging within me. I listened up the stairs for any sounds of little feet running around — the kids were sound asleep. I went to the bars on the weekends. My kids were safe with a babysitter, and I felt free to dance, drink and mingle. I normally didn't entertain men when the kids were home, but maybe this was it. No more one-night stands. Maybe he was the one I'd been looking for all this time. I smoothed down my hair and opened the door, grinning my most charming smile.

"Hi, Dillon," I cooed, hoping he couldn't see my shaking hands. My heart pounded against my ribs, and I wondered if he could hear it thundering.

"Hey, Bella." His voice slid like silk across my skin. His eyes drew me in like a gentle caress. "Sorry it's so late, but I can't stop thinking about you. Last week was amazing, and I just had to see you again. Can I come in?"

I opened the door and invited him in. As soon as the door closed, he turned to me, and his eyes turned cold and hard.

"So, what do you want to do?" I asked sweetly.

"I ... I don't know," he stuttered, his eyes darting across the room and up the stairs.

New BEGINNINGS

Suddenly he began pacing the house. Prowling like an animal on the hunt, he searched the house with the eyes of a wild tiger. He was checking the house, making sure we were alone. Eventually those hungry eyes settled on the prey they were waiting for — me. In the blink of an eye, the kind, charming man I thought I knew became a monster intent on ravaging both my body and my home. Again and again he stole what I had freely given on so many occasions.

"Stop it!" I screamed, crawling to the door. But he was too quick. He grabbed me again and threw me on the ground. Like the defeated dragged by a victor, I fell limp with hopelessness. There was no way out of this nightmare. Nowhere to run and nowhere to hide. But didn't I deserve this? This is what I deserved for bringing men I barely knew home from the bar.

"You're not getting away, Bella. Not until I'm done with you." His warm breath slid over me, and my stomach churned in disgust.

Please, stop this. Please let someone come. My mind cried out to God.

But no one came.

I knew I had to get away. I ran across the kitchen, but Dillon caught me just as I reached the top of the basement stairs. His eyes pierced me with the fury of a wild beast. I held onto the handrails as he tried to push me down the stairs. I knew the fall could break my neck, but my strength was nothing compared to the man towering over me.

THE ONE

"God, help me!" I screamed. "If I get out of this, I'll go back to church! I'll stop drinking and sleeping around. Just please help!"

As Dillon reached forward to push me down the steep stairs, an invisible force swelled in front of me. Like a brick wall, something stood before my shaking body, protecting me from the strength of the monster behind me. Although he pushed with all his might, he could not push me down the stairs. Some stronger force stood in front of me, protecting me from certain death.

Finally, Dillon surrendered, but the evil gleam in his eyes never left. He slammed the door, leaving me in the darkness of the staircase. I could hear the scraping of something big being dragged across the kitchen floor. I suddenly realized he was moving the refrigerator in front of the door to the staircase.

I was trapped in my own home, with a maniac on the loose.

Panic seized me as I realized my children were upstairs still sleeping. *What would he do to them?* I had to escape. With a strength not my own, I put my hands on the door and pushed the refrigerator out of the way. I walked out, squinting at the brightness of the lights. I could see Dillon's silhouette as he ran out the door with my purse and money.

Relief washed over me, and I crumpled to the floor. My body shook from exhaustion, fear and adrenaline, but knowing my kids were safe upstairs in their beds caused tears of joy to flood my eyes.

New BEGINNINGS

"Thank you, God," I breathed. It was over, and I had a promise to keep.

☙☙☙

I sat on the steps of my house, wishing I could disappear into the cold, hard cement. The visitors had come and gone, and I was alone with my grief. Abby was the last to leave, and with her fading footsteps, my final shred of hope slipped away. At 30 years old, I'd lost my beautiful mother to a stroke, and I felt completely alone. No parents, no grandparents, no husband. I was raising three kids by myself, and I felt utterly and completely alone. The loneliness threatened to swallow me whole, and once again, thoughts of worthlessness assailed my fragile mind.

You're horrible, Bella. Look at your life. You're all alone, and nobody wants you. What makes you think you deserve any better? You don't deserve to be happy. You definitely don't deserve anything from God.

After the nightmare with Dillon, I'd kept my word, hoping that it would help me finally turn my life around. We found a church, and before long, it felt like we had found a family. I stopped drinking, but I was far from free. My relationship with God teetered like a seesaw dependent on my feelings. Back and forth I bounced, with one foot in and one foot out. When the church split, my feelings of abandonment returned, and I felt as if I were drowning in disappointment.

THE ONE

It was just another relationship that let me down. Why did I expect anything different?

In my loneliness, I flew like a moth back to the neon lights of the bars. Their twinkling eyes danced in the night sky, beckoning me like a lighthouse. I knew all the right answers from my years in church. God would help me through this if I simply turned to him. But the lure of security in the arms of a man beckoned me once again to the shadows of the night. Maybe I wouldn't find someone forever, but I could find someone for tonight. Maybe he wouldn't stay for tomorrow, but I would have someone next to me for today. Besides, they liked me. I knew how to play the part. I could be whoever they wanted me to be, and that was just fine by me.

I drowned my sorrows in the bottle, sighing as the liquid slid down my throat, warming my belly. I escaped my fears by giving into the desires of my flesh. All the stress of work crept away with every drink. All the hopeless thoughts retreated to the shadows with every stranger's embrace. Why stay sober when I could laugh and dance in the freedom of another drink? Yet when the morning light broke through the haze of night, I was alone. And there in the light of day, I faced once again the undeniable emptiness of life.

꙳꙳꙳

My eyes drooped as I stared blankly at the computer screen. The silence permeating the computer lab made

New BEGINNINGS

each click of the keyboard patter like rain against a window. The chorus of keyboards across the room sang around me, while the constant pounding of my heart sounded like a gong announcing my failures to the world. I was taking college classes to get my life on track, but I couldn't shake the nagging depression that followed me like an ominous storm cloud. My life was so far from what I dreamed it would be. So many shattered dreams lay scattered across my past. I wondered where God was in all of it. Had he forsaken me? Did he even care? The sensible part of me concluded that he didn't. Why else would I still be here, trying to dig myself out of the mess of life?

From deep within, I felt a voice speak to me. It wasn't audible, but I believe it was God speaking.

My precious child, the voice whispered to my soul. *I am taking care of you, even though you have forgotten about me. I am here, waiting for you to come to me. Stop running away. You are mine, and I love you.*

Tears poured down my face. I was tired of running. I was tired of wallowing in my guilt. I realized that all the things I was doing to escape reality were just more shackles. I wanted freedom. Not the freedom to dance the night away. No — I wanted a freedom that stayed the next day.

I started looking for churches. One by one, I noticed a similar message, and I believe God was speaking to me again. No matter what church I went to, one question was always asked. *Where is your commitment to God?* I couldn't answer this question because I was never

THE ONE

committed to God. I was committed to finding happiness and love, but I wasn't committed to God. The guilt I carried with me dragged like an anchor around my neck, marking a jagged path through the sand. I could look back and see every fall, every setback and every mistake. I knew I needed to let it go. I needed to get back to the basics of what my mom and grandma had taught me so many years before. Jesus died to give me life. I was never made to carry the weight of my mistakes. I could give them to Jesus, and he would set me free.

When I found myself at Trinity Full Gospel, I knew I had come home. The people were so kind and caring, and the wall around my heart began to crumble with their friendship and acceptance. One night as the pastor preached, his words shot like a bullet straight at me.

"Sometimes, we just have to get back to the basics," he said as if speaking directly to me.

"Oh, God," I cried. "I've gone all over the place, looking for what will make me whole. I've forgotten about you, but I'm coming back. Please forgive me! I can't do this alone. I'm too broken. But I believe you died to pay the price for my depravity. Take me, and make me yours alone!"

Soon after, I recommitted my life to Christ, and in front of my church family, I was baptized — dipped in water as an outward sign of how God washed away the filth in me. I started reading the Bible and began to get to know God and his passionate pursuit of my heart. One day, during church, my pastor came up to me and told me

New BEGINNINGS

that someone in my family had prayed to the Lord a long time ago, and my generation would see the answers to those prayers. I knew he was talking about my grandma Frances and my mom. Because they never stopped praying or believing, I was finally coming back. Yes, it had been a long, grueling road, but in his faithfulness, God was always bringing me back home to his arms. Now it was time to build on the foundation my grandma and mother had built. It was time to pick up the shattered fragments of my broken dreams and discover the purpose God had for me. His plans for me still take my breath away.

A new hunger began to grow within me. The gaping hole within me closed once I finally began filling my mind with the truth. As I read my Bible, God swept me off my feet. I couldn't get enough of him, and his words poured like rain over a dry, deserted wasteland. He showed me who I am — *his beloved.* I was so busy pretending to be whoever people wanted me to be that I never took the time to find out who I really am. Through the pages of the Bible, God showed me that I'm worth something, not because I have anything to offer, but simply because he made me, and he loves me. As I got to know him, I got to know myself. For when I see my reflection in his eyes, I see a love that makes my knees go weak.

Little by little, I began surrendering the deepest parts of my heart to God. When the sadness came, I told him. When the thoughts of all my mistakes bombarded me, I ran to him. When those feelings of worthlessness and the desire to kill myself overwhelmed me, I turned to the truth

THE ONE

of who I am in him. For my entire life, I'd allowed the lies to saturate my mind, until they became my reality. I realized that the truth of God's love for me was the only thing that could set me free.

※※※

One Sunday after the morning service at Trinity Full Gospel, I confessed to my friend Jamie my lingering feelings of insecurity. Ever since I was a little girl, I wanted a man to swoop in and rescue me. I wanted a man to want me enough to marry me. I always thought that once I found this perfect relationship, I would finally be happy.

"I know that God is with me," I told her, "but sometimes I still feel alone."

"When I was growing up, I went to church and tried to do the right thing," she said sweetly. "I knew God, but he felt far away. Then I went on a mission trip to Panama, and on my trip I realized that a relationship with God is very personal, almost like being married to him. My dad gave me a ring on my 16th birthday, and I'm pretty sure that was God's way of telling me that he is real and with me all the time. Marriage was a broken thing for me, since my parents had divorced, but God used this ring to heal my heart and make me fall in love with him!"

"That's the kind of relationship I want. For so long, I've wanted a man beside me. To hold me when I've felt lonely. But you're right. Jamie, I just want God to cover me with his love!"

"All you have to do is ask him!" she said, smiling.

New BEGINNINGS

୶୶୶

The steam rose from my coffee, and I breathed in the rich aroma, letting the warmth wash over me. I sat on my front porch, basking in the rays of the morning sun, reflecting on all that God has done in my life.

"God, it's so good to sit here and relax with you," I whispered, inner butterflies fluttering at the thought of him smiling down on me.

The wind began to blow, as if in response. It whirled around me, and in it I felt the fingers of God caressing my face, running through my hair. What a thrill to be loved so deeply by the one who daily chases my heart.

Working two jobs, moments like these were rare. I learned to sit with God no matter how busily the world swirls around me. I learned he's there in the stress of work. He's there in the tears of loneliness. He's there as I spin and run with the craziness of life.

I raised my three children by myself. They are grown now, and God is working in their lives. He's reaching in, sewing back together the broken fragments of their childhoods — weaving together a beautiful tapestry of grace and hope.

In all my wandering and running, I always looked for the one who would make my dreams come true. In my desperation, I looked in all the wrong places. I didn't know who I was apart from my mistakes and failures. But God gave me a joy beyond my wildest dreams. Because of the blood of Jesus, I don't have to ever believe the lies again. I

THE ONE

am forgiven and free. God is refreshing and renewing me. I no longer see the Bible as just a bunch of stories. They became real, life-breathing truths with the power to heal a broken heart.

God filled the hidden crevices of my heart — the places I didn't even know were there. I became free from the guilt, the shame, the worthlessness and the loneliness that haunted me for so many years.

Although life isn't easy, I learned to trust that I am safe in God's presence.

After talking with Jamie, I asked God again for the one thing I'd always wanted — love and acceptance. I knew that God loved me deeper, higher and wider than any human could ever love someone. I wanted to fall more in love with him than I ever had before.

Swallowing my pride, I fell to my knees and asked, "Jesus, will *you* marry me?"

Shortly after, I went on a mission trip with my church. We served on a Native American reservation. At the market one day, I stood beside my pastor's wife, admiring the beautiful Indian hairpieces. I hesitated to purchase anything, but Barb decided to buy one for me. I thanked her for her kindness. I had really wanted one.

When we returned from the trip, a friend saw the hairpiece and asked me if I knew what it represented.

"No." I shook my head.

"It represents the union of marriage, when a man and a woman become one. A hair covering means you are taken."

New BEGINNINGS

Goose bumps covered my skin, and the hair on my arms rose as understanding flooded my heart. Tears dropped from my eyes, and I struggled to catch my breath.

And then I heard a voice deep in my spirit — the voice of a groom madly in love with his bride.

Bella. My darling Bella. Of course I want to marry you. I've always wanted to marry you.

I once thought that the arms of a man would make me feel whole, but instead they left me damaged and empty. The arms of God, the lover of my soul, are the ones I've been waiting for all my life. He covers me. He makes me whole. He won't ever let me go.

SPEECHLESS
The Story of Dave
Written by Marty Minchin

I stood at the Dairy Queen counter, mulling over my options. Chocolate. Vanilla. Hot Fudge. Strawberry. The air conditioning inside the restaurant was a welcome relief from the hot summer sun outside, and a milkshake would only make it better.

I loved milkshakes.

My childhood home in Zanesville, Ohio, was down the road from the Dairy Queen and close enough to walk to. I had loved milkshakes since I was a young child, and as I grew older, my fondness for the cold, creamy treats grew with me.

I'd spent the day trolling the neighborhood, looking for yards where the grass was long enough to need cutting. Every yard mowed equaled money in the bank for my milkshake fund, which needed to stretch the whole year until the rain and heat of the spring made the grass grow again.

My dad made a decent living as a tool and die maker at a factory, but our family only could afford to eat out on Friday nights, if that. If I wanted to buy extras like milkshakes at Dairy Queen, I had to pay for them. Sometimes I craved several a day.

"I'll have hot fudge," I told the cashier, finally deciding on my favorite flavor. I laid the cash on the counter.

New BEGINNINGS

There has to be an easier way to earn money.

In my driveway at home, there was parked a $400 Opal Manta sports car that my dad had helped me buy after my 16th birthday. "Freedom" might as well have been emblazoned on its side, because that little car was making me dream way beyond my neighbors' yards.

With a car, I could drive to a job. I'd put an application in at McDonald's, and the paycheck there would, of course, buy plenty of milkshakes. But the way I calculated it, there would be a little money left over.

I sucked down the milkshake as I walked down the road and thought about my life. I didn't know much about what the world outside held for a teenage boy. All I knew was that I was ready for a taste of it.

❧❧❧

After they got married, my parents settled into the house where they lived when my sister and I were born. We bordered on a low-income housing community, but our neighborhood was comfortable and safe. My dad worked the nightshift, and when he wasn't sleeping during the day, he was helping out at a gas station he owned with his brother in a nearby town.

Mom and Dad hadn't strayed far from our extended family. Both sets of my grandparents lived in town, and some cousins were close by in Michigan. Our weekends and vacations involved visiting relatives, whether it was summers at my grandparents' house, where I learned to

SPEECHLESS

cook, or trips to Atlanta to spend time with my uncle. Sundays were Dad's only day off, and when he got up, he was either working on a car or helping someone with home repairs. Otherwise, at least part of the day was spent with a set of grandparents. Often we'd been with my other grandparents the night before, where my parents played cards with them after dinner.

When I was 7 years old, I fell in love with baseball. If the game was in season, I was on a team. I often joined two or three leagues at a time playing outfield, pitcher or catcher. If I wasn't on the baseball diamond, I was riding my bike in the neighborhood until the streetlights came on and I knew it was time to come in and eat. Even then, Mom often had to warm up my dinner for me. There was always a game of whiffle ball or baseball going on in the churchyard behind the house or a group of kids from another neighborhood to take on in football.

Despite the normalcy of my childhood, a lingering sadness hung around our house like an early-morning haze. My mom had lost two baby boys, each about a week after they'd been born prematurely five months into her pregnancies. She rarely talked about them, but the joy of my brother's birth — 12 years after mine — cleared the fog like a ray of bright sunlight. As soon as my little brother could walk, I took him out in the backyard and taught him how to play whiffle ball. By the time he was old enough to join a league, he was practically a pro.

My job at McDonald's cut into my time with my family. At first I cooked over the grill and cleaned the

New BEGINNINGS

fryers, but as I earned my boss' trust, he gave me keys to the restaurant and asked me to close a few nights a week. I'd seen my co-workers head off together after the restaurant closed on the weekends, and it wasn't long before they invited me to join them.

❦❦❦

"Hey, Dave! The beer's in the cooler. Help yourself." Jeff, my co-worker, turned back to his conversation, and I eyed the blue top of the Igloo ice chest.

I'd barely stepped in the door of the trailer, which apparently was the after-hours gathering place for McDonald's employees. My co-workers relaxed on couches, talking and downing beer as easily as glasses of cold water on a hot day. I surveyed the crowd. Most people were older, and the few guys I knew from school clearly were not first-time drinkers.

Don't be a stick in the mud. Don't be a stick in the mud.

I took a deep breath and reached into the cooler. The only parties with drinking I'd been to were a few weenie roasts with my parents, and there was no way I was going to not drink a beer at this one and look like a dork.

The beer bottle was cold in my hand. I took a swig, and with a monumental effort I choked the liquid down and kept my face from looking like I'd bitten into a lemon.

The second and third swallows went down a little more smoothly and surprisingly started to seem almost

SPEECHLESS

natural. I felt myself loosen up, grabbed another bottle and another, and as I drank my fifth beer, I was laughing too loudly at the drunk Chihuahua that had lapped up the beer someone poured in its water dish.

One beer later, I became the Chihuahua.

I stumbled around, hearing the rumbling voices around me as they jokingly compared me to the little dog that couldn't walk a straight line. They all knew it was my first time drinking, and some offered a sympathetic pat on the back when I emerged from the bathroom after a long session bowing down to the porcelain throne.

❧❧❧

I could have said no to the steady stream of invitations to drink at the trailer after closing, but the get-togethers were fun. Until then, all of my friends had been either cousins who lived across the street or other kids in the neighborhood. I had buddies at school, but we didn't hang out after the afternoon bell rang. The McDonald's crowd was older and interesting, and drinking late into the night became a regular part of my routine. I liked playing cards with them, and they knew good jokes and how to have a good time. My neighborhood friends mostly wanted to ride bikes, go to the mall or sit around and do nothing. I was the only one of the group who could drive and had a car, and hanging around with them got old.

Soon, my nights out with my co-workers stretched into the early morning, and I was sneaking into the house just a few hours before Dad got up for work.

New BEGINNINGS

My nightlife was easy to hide from my parents. I'd always been good about calling and telling them where I was, and they assumed I came straight home from McDonald's. Mom spent most of her energy in the mornings trying to get my sister out of bed, and I'd hop up just in time to run downstairs and make a quick trip to the bathroom to comb my hair and put on deodorant before heading out the door.

Sometimes I'd go to school with a hangover after being out all night. I learned to control myself enough not to throw up, but the alcohol drained my energy and gave me headaches. My parents never seemed to know the difference.

☙☙☙

I'd met my first girlfriend in sixth grade. She lived four streets up, and we'd started talking as we walked home from school one day. In the summer between sixth and seventh grades, she moved away, but we bounced back and forth like a rubber ball until high school. We'd lose touch, and then she'd call and we'd be back together. Mom would drop me off at her house for a few hours on the weekends, and we'd reconnect. A few months later, she'd break up with me over the phone. I thought she was my one true love, so I always took her back. Until I met Vanessa.

Vanessa sat down at my lunch table one day halfway through my senior year in high school. She was thin and

SPEECHLESS

blond with eyes that narrowed when she smiled, and half the guys at the table wanted to date her. Vanessa was new to our school, but I didn't bother to ask her how old she was. She carried herself with a confidence that I liked. Her jokes made me laugh, and she partied as much as I did, although she preferred her friends to the McDonald's crowd. I thought I loved her.

In June of 1986, I graduated from high school, and Vanessa moved about 30 miles away to live with her dad. When I had a day off work, I'd drive up and go out with Vanessa and her friends or hang out at her dad's apartment.

She called me before one of my visits to tell me we needed to talk. I didn't think much of it, but my happiness at seeing her fizzled like a flat soft drink before I even stepped in the door. Her bad mood was palpable.

"Sit down," Vanessa said, motioning toward the kitchen. By this time, her dad had lost his apartment, and they were living with some friends.

We faced each other across someone else's breakfast table.

"I'm pregnant." She scowled.

My heart leapt. "I'm going to be a father?" I couldn't stop the smile spreading across my face.

I had always known I'd wanted to be a dad. I'd helped raise my younger brother, and I looked forward to having kids of my own.

Why does she look so angry?

Vanessa was 15 years old and living with her alcoholic

New BEGINNINGS

father because he was a better choice than her mom and stepdad. She wanted to finish high school, and caring for a baby did not fit in with her plans for sophomore year. Her lost childhood was flashing through her mind; my future as a dad and husband was taking shape in mine.

What I knew of marriage came from my parents' long relationship, so there was no question I would do the right thing and marry Vanessa after she turned 16. Her dad threw a little bit of a fit when we told him, but that subsided into relief when he realized it meant he'd no longer have to raise her. He agreed to sign the papers authorizing Vanessa, as a minor, to get married, and we tied the knot in the front room of a preacher Mom arranged for the ceremony. Vanessa and I met with him a few times for counseling, but I barely remembered his name or whether he worked at a church in town. My parents, brother and sister attended our wedding ceremony, and then I moved Vanessa back to Zanesville to live in our new apartment.

Our drinking and partying slowed down while she was pregnant, but after Zack was born, we started going out together again. That lasted about six months, and then we realized it would be easier to bring the party to us. We'd put Zack to bed, and our friends would stream in and fill up the couches. Most nights the group was her friends, but occasionally a few of mine would pop in.

In a spurt of responsibility, I quit my job at McDonald's and looked for a "real job." Jobs were easy to find but hard to keep, especially when I kept drinking so much at night that I was late for work the next day. I laid carpet, drove a forklift, worked in a factory and delivered furniture for a Rent-A-Center.

Vanessa had tried to go back to high school, but as her belly got bigger she couldn't stand the idea that people might be talking about her. She dropped out before Zack was born. She worked at a big-box store in Zanesville, but she still had plenty of time to spend with the boyfriend she had on the side.

By the time our daughter Lilly was born in 1990, our patterns were well established. I stayed home with the kids and drank with my friend while she went out, usually with her boyfriend and her friends. I knew exactly who the guy was. She had dated him before me, and now his mom was dating her dad. They snuck around at first, but after a while they didn't even bother to hide it. He'd call all the time in the middle of the night, and when I answered the phone, he and I would fight and argue.

Still, I tried to keep the marriage together even as the wheels fell off of it. My parents had been together for years, and I didn't really know what divorce was. When you married someone, I thought, you stayed together forever. I knew that between my drinking and series of jobs I wasn't the greatest of husbands, but I was willing to put up with almost anything Vanessa did to be with Zack and Lilly.

I made plans with Vanessa to go out on her birthday, one of my feeble attempts to fan the dying embers of our marriage. She promptly canceled. When her boyfriend

New BEGINNINGS

and friend came to pick her up for the night instead, I almost exploded.

When we ran out of words to scream at each other, Vanessa jumped on my back like a monkey, flailing at my head and shoulders with her arms. I spun around to shake her off, feeling the blood coming out of my ears and my broken glasses hanging off my face. I swung my head back to dislodge her, and as our skulls crashed she slid off to the floor and ran out the door. I knew he was waiting for her in the car.

Ten minutes later, Vanessa and her crew returned with a police officer.

I explained my side of the story.

"She called first," the cop replied.

I spent the night in jail and walked home the next morning. The front door was locked, and when I leaned closer, I could hear him moving around inside. I banged on the door.

"Let me in, Vanessa! I live here, too! I'm going to call the cops if you don't open the door."

Silence.

I trudged over to my sister's house. When Vanessa finally picked up the phone, she agreed to let me come home the next day. The boyfriend was gone, but when I opened the lid of the washing machine, some of his laundry was still there.

Vanessa and I settled down a little, but we argued and fought, and she refused to give up her boyfriend. After one particularly long night of fighting, I dragged myself to the

SPEECHLESS

dentist's office to have my wisdom teeth pulled. I fell into bed at home to sleep off the anesthesia. When I woke up, I headed to the bathroom and passed out when I sat on the toilet. I struggled to stand up when I came to, and I fell down again.

I heard a car door shut outside and glanced out the window. Vanessa hopped out of a car, and I could see the guy and her friends inside. Vanessa bounced in the door, and I told her about what had happened.

"Idiot." She turned away, laughing.

"It wasn't funny. I could have cracked my head open."

Another argument erupted. Vanessa cocked her fist and punched me in the nose. My first instinct was to hit her back, but I let my fist fly by her head and into the wall.

I slowly pulled my arm back, rubbing my knuckles. This had gone too far.

༄༄༄

I didn't want to ever actually hit Vanessa, and I didn't want to go back to jail. This wasn't working, and it was time to walk away.

"You need to take your stuff and go to your dad's where you can cool down." Vanessa's voice was cold. By this time, Mom and Dad had divorced after 20 years of marriage, and Dad had a small house nearby.

"You know what, I'm tired of fighting." I couldn't be in this marriage anymore. "I'm going to my dad's and not coming back."

New BEGINNINGS

I packed what I could during the time it took Dad to drive over, and I left with what I could carry. I'm not sure what happened to the rest of it.

I never went back to the house I shared with Vanessa, but we spent more than a year untangling ourselves from each other. She and the kids moved in with her boyfriend and his mom, but we still talked on and off. I clung to the shards of our relationship, regardless of how sharp they were. Vanessa held out reconciliation like a worm on a hook, and if she wanted to talk or get together, I'd do whatever I could to accommodate her. She had our kids, and if I had to bend over backward to be with them, I'd do it.

When she asked me to meet her during her lunch break from work one day, I quickly agreed.

I had Zack and Lilly for the day, so the four of us met at a restaurant. I caught a glimpse of her boyfriend watching the kids and me from his car on the other side of the parking lot, but he wasn't trying to keep his presence a secret. He barreled out of the car toward the restaurant, running his mouth as I tried to hustle the kids in the door.

A sharp pain broke through the chaos as my head snapped to the side. He had sucker punched me and taken off, and all I could do was yell at his back as he retreated across the parking lot.

"We're done," I told Vanessa. "Let's get on with the divorce."

Divorce was so foreign to me that I was too naïve to even read the papers her lawyer served me. I didn't know I

SPEECHLESS

was entitled to visitation rights, so Vanessa took the kids and let me have them whenever she needed a babysitter. If I'd gone over the divorce agreement, I would have known that I should have had the kids on holidays and regularly on weekends. As it was, however, visitation depended on Vanessa's whims. She was pretty good about letting me see the kids on Sundays, but there were many holidays she agreed to let me have them, but then called a few hours later and told me to bring them back.

Zack and Lilly were a welcome distraction when they were allowed to come over. Even though they were toddlers, I treated them like friends. While Vanessa was out with her friends and boyfriend, Zack and I would play Duck Hunt on my PlayStation. I'd crack open a beer, give Zack a gun controller that wasn't plugged in and let him shoot away at the ducks on the screen. We'd play in my dad's backyard or walk around the mall and get something to eat. Fatherhood was turning out to be as fun as I'd hoped.

The kids weren't around that much, however, and in their absence depression crept in. I had nothing better to do than drink and party, and it was easy to grab a case of beer after I got off second shift at the embroidery company I was working for and head over to a friend's house. Sometimes we'd pass around a joint, but I never liked marijuana enough to buy a stash for myself. For about six months, I subsisted on bean burritos from Taco Bell and beer. I lost about 50 pounds along with any sense of hope.

New BEGINNINGS

My divorce became final in 1992, and soon after I got laid off from my job. I hadn't worked there long, and I only qualified for a few months of unemployment.

In all of those years I'd been a regular at Dairy Queen, I'd never noticed the hole-in-the-wall bar across the street. I could cut through a couple of backyards from my dad's house and be at the bar in less than 10 minutes, and I never had to step foot on a major road. Over the next few months, I went to that bar so much that I'm surprised there wasn't a path worn through our neighbors' grass.

The bar was about the size of a one-bedroom apartment, and the action revolved around a horseshoe-shaped bar. The food was good, and before long I was seated at a table there every day ordering a cheeseburger and fries for lunch. The place drew me like a magnet, and I walked there whether it was beautiful and sunny or cold and rainy.

The main attraction was Kelly, a barmaid I'd taken a fancy to. It didn't seem to matter that she was married, and we started sneaking around while her husband was at work.

She'd stop by my dad's house to be with me on her way to work in the mornings, and then I'd head to the bar after I got up and moving around. I'd hang out, drink and play pool with the guys in the pool league that met there. Sometimes I played well. Other times I'd had so much beer that I couldn't hold a pool stick steady. I staggered out of the bar around 1 a.m., its closing time, almost every morning, and if I was too drunk to walk, I'd crawl through an alley back to Dad's house. One time a skunk chased me down that alley all the way home.

My unemployment money quickly ran out, but my drinking habit was going strong. Thanks to Kelly and, strangely enough, her husband, I rarely paid for a drink at the bar. She'd either carry my bar tab or slip me money after she got off work so that I could keep drinking. Her husband hung out at the bar, too, and we got to be good friends. He either didn't know about his wife's affair or didn't care. Some nights he'd swing by the bar to pick me up to party at a different bar. His company had gone out of business, and he'd received a sizable settlement, so he always bought our drinks. If Kelly came with us, I'd pick up another woman at whatever bar we went to. I woke up many mornings in a strange bed with a strange woman beside me. Sometimes I knew her name, but many times I didn't.

※※※

Money became more and more of a problem. The little bit I had went toward gas and beer. I spent Christmas Eve with my dad that year, and as we sat and chatted, he asked me what I'd gotten the kids for Christmas.

"Nothing." I shrugged. "I don't have any money."

"Are you kidding?" Dad let me have it for neglecting Zack and Lilly before ushering me to the car. We made a late-night run to the store to pick up a few presents from each of us, and I stood next to my dad at the cash register

New BEGINNINGS

like a little kid as he pulled out his credit card and paid for everything.

With no job, I had to find another source of income. That came in the form of Longaberger baskets.

I'd seen the little handmade wooden baskets at friends' houses, and I knew that women paid a lot of money for them at those home shopping parties. I'd also heard you could get a good price for them at a pawnshop.

When I wasn't at the bar, I went to my dad's neighbors' house to drink and play cards. I scoped out one Longaberger basket next to their curio cabinet and one next to the front door. We usually sat around a table in the kitchen, and when I got ready to leave one night, they headed upstairs to check on their kids. It was so easy to pick up those baskets and walk out the front door, my mind on the beer and gas I could buy in the coming week.

I also found things to steal and sell from my dad's house. I lifted some of his tools and a gun, but when I tried to pawn it, the shop owner looked up the registration. It came back to my dad, who promptly kicked me out of his house when he found out I was stealing from him.

My 1980 Chevy Chevette became the roof over my head. Dad would let me come in and shower when he got home from work, but then he put me right back out the door. I pulled the car next to Dad's garage, just barely out of sight of the house. With the car in park, I'd lay back the driver's seat and try to sleep bent at the awkward angle of the reclined seat. I could see in a window of the house from my front seat, and in the mornings I'd watch him getting ready for work and think about me sitting outside, sad, in my car, because of the choices I'd made. As if he could hear my thoughts, Dad sometimes looked back out at me and shook his head in disgust. I was too embarrassed to meet his gaze.

The bar was getting expensive, so I now spent many nights with neighborhood friends and renewed an acquaintance with a woman I'd met through Vanessa. She was married, but her husband was away at boot camp for the U.S. Army, and she felt free to hang out with me. We played putt-putt golf together, and then she invited me over to drink. I drove down to her house with Dad's girlfriend's son Jake, looking forward to the prospect of a few beers.

Ellen had a young kid, and she was worried that if we all got drunk no one would be capable of caring for him in the morning. She called a babysitter, and Jake left to pick her up. He returned with a beautiful teenage girl with long, curly brown hair.

I elbowed Jake when he sat down next to me. "She's going to be my next ex-wife," I joked, although I wasn't really joking. There was something about this girl, who was full of energy, happy and giddy.

We drank and partied late into the night, and everyone fell asleep except Cara, the babysitter, and me. I didn't have much on my mind except sleeping with her, but as we talked we figured out that she knew my kids because her best friend's mother used to babysit them. Cara didn't party, and she told me things about my Zack and Lilly that

New BEGINNINGS

I didn't even know. I'd been with a lot of women since Vanessa and I had split, but I'd never connected with one over the kids.

The conversation I had with Cara blossomed into a dating relationship, even though she was only 17 and about to enter her senior year in high school. Instead of going to high school parties or spending time with her school friends, she'd give up her weekends to be with me, Zack and Lilly, almost like a family of four. I wasn't that much older than her, after all, and I liked spending time with her.

On October 14, 1993, the fragile world I was building with Cara fell apart. I was staying with her sister, and someone knocked on her door. I could see through the window that it was a police officer, so I didn't answer it.

Cara found out a detective was looking for me, and she refused to let me ignore whatever I needed to own up to. I had told this innocent girl nothing about my past, and she seemed as mystified as I was pretending to be.

"You've got to go talk to that detective," she told me. "It could be important."

My stomach filled with dread. Whatever it was, it couldn't be good.

Cara and her dad accompanied me to the police station, but the detective sent them home without me. I went straight to jail, accused of breaking and entering, theft and forgery. The owners of the Longaberger baskets had figured out what happened to them.

This was not my first night in jail, of course. I'd been

SPEECHLESS

jailed after the fight with Vanessa, and I'd spent 30 days locked up once because I fell behind in child support. This time, though, a new life dangled before me like a bright red apple growing at the end of a branch. I had been climbing out to get it, stopped short by the possibility of five to 25 years in prison.

Why me? I had just started straightening up!

I thought about Cara during the two weeks I waited for the date of my court appearance, but not about the future we likely wouldn't have. She graciously accepted my many collect phone calls, and she wrote me a letter every day. One time when I called, she was standing in for me on my visitation day with the kids. Why on earth was this kind, caring girl still with me?

My court date finally arrived, and I shuffled into the courtroom to face my fate. My head jerked up in surprise when the judge announced that the couple had dropped the breaking and entering charge after admitting to police that they had invited me into their home that night.

The charges of theft and forgery stood, but the sentence was doable. I took a plea bargain for two and a half years of jail time. When I was transferred to a reception center from the county jail, I was told that I could go through a boot camp for first-time offenders for 90 days, spend 30 days in a halfway house and then go home on parole instead of being away for two and a half years. The future had begun to open up again, and I dreamed about what could be.

First there was Cara. She was now taking the kids on

New BEGINNINGS

all of my visitation days. She had them for Thanksgiving and Christmas and bought them gifts. All I could think about was enduring my months of penance and getting back to her.

If she loves my kids that much, she must love me that much, too.

Cara was not going to be my next *ex*-wife. I wanted to marry her, forever.

☙☙☙

We planned for a spring wedding, but Cara's parents wouldn't let her live with me before we were married, so we moved our date up. We found out two months before the wedding that Cara was pregnant. I shaped up for a while, checking in with my parole officer once a week, taking random breathalyzer and drug tests and, at 25 years old, sticking to my state-imposed midnight curfew.

I got out on parole early, but the state of Ohio had deemed me an alcoholic and required me to go to Alcoholics Anonymous meetings for 18 months as part of my parole. By that time, I'd started drinking again, mostly at home — other than when I grabbed a few beers with Cara at the restaurant across the street from the warehouse that hosted my AA group.

AA meetings bored me. About 20 of us would sit around a long table in what looked like a boiler room freshened up with a coffee pot and cookies in the corner. I'd look around at the other people sharing their sob stories and watch the secondhand on the wall clock ticking off the slowest 30 minutes in history. If the leader called on me to tell my story, I'd pass. Why share my life with a bunch of strangers?

Our daughter was born in March, and as soon as Cara was up for it, I began inviting her to go to the bars with me. We met up with guys I knew in high school, and before I knew it our weekend nights out bled over into the weeknights. My schedule changed when I began a new job working from 2 to 11 p.m. at a children's home, and Cara would be asleep when I got off. I found a new group to go out with.

Old habits can be hard to kick, and one night I met a woman at a bar who piqued my interest. We got to talking, and I was drunk and went home with her. I'm not even sure if I asked her name.

We left the bar and went to her apartment somewhere in downtown Zanesville. Afterward, I felt really guilty, so I slunk out and quietly went back home in the middle of the night.

Cara woke up and realized that I was not home. She called friends and family and even went out looking for me, but couldn't find me. When I got home that night, she was very angry, and we fought in the yard. We went back up to the apartment and went to bed. The next morning she asked me who I had been with, but I couldn't even remember fighting in the yard with her. I denied having done anything wrong and told her that I was at a friend's playing cards.

What had I done?

New BEGINNINGS

❧❧❧

"Have you slept with someone else?" Cara asked one day shortly after.

I was terrified that the truth would mean the end of our marriage.

"Of course not."

"Are you sure?" she asked.

"Look, Cara, I'm not sleeping around, okay? I haven't done anything."

She gave me a funny look, but she backed off. The topic didn't come up again for another four years. Those years I was tormented by what I had done, and it took a terrible toll on our relationship.

We had another baby in 1998, but even a second child couldn't bridge the growing void between us. I was consumed with guilt and shame for what I had done to her. We'd sit in a room together for hours and hardly talk. We would go weeks, and then months, without being together in the bedroom. When bedtime came, I'd often make excuses to stay up while she went up to our room alone. I couldn't stop speculating about what she was thinking about me.

I didn't trust myself to go out to bars anymore, so I limited my drinking to home. A friend would come over on Friday and Saturday nights, and we'd have a few beers together.

I took a job as a truck driver, thinking absence might make our hearts grow fonder. On the road, I'd happily imagine the joyful reunion we'd have when I got home, but I couldn't translate the plans in my head into reality, and I'd make more excuses about why I couldn't go to bed with Cara.

The silence between us went on for eight years.

☙☙☙

"You are going to get up right now and come to church with me."

I opened my eyes and saw Cara, dressed up, staring down at me next to the bed.

"What?" I rubbed my face and willed myself out of my hangover. I'd been drinking in the living room until 3 a.m. Cara didn't vocalize an ultimatum, but it silently hung over my head: no church, no marriage.

Earlier, she had finally gotten the truth out of me.

"Can I ask you a question?" We were lying together in bed.

"Yes."

"Will you tell me the truth?"

"Well, yeah."

"Did you have an affair?"

My heart beat so loudly in my chest, I was afraid she would hear it. All I could picture was her packing her bags and leaving. I took a breath.

"Yes, I did."

We laid in the silence and cried together. She told me she forgave me, but I couldn't forgive myself.

New BEGINNINGS

Cara had grown up in a church, and she knew how to talk to God. She'd begun attending Trinity Full Gospel Church on Sundays. I knew she had been asking God for something to change in our marriage. For the time being, she seemed content with me just going to church, regardless of what state of mind I was in. I lumbered out of bed, put on some half-decent clothes and joined her in the car.

Nothing at church made sense to me. I listened to the singing and the pastor's teaching, but I didn't understand much of what he said. I went to church every Sunday with Cara, but a few hours after the service ended, I couldn't recount the sermon topic.

On the other hand, I liked the people I met at church. They never asked me about my bloodshot eyes or the scent of alcohol that sometimes followed me around the building. They always seemed happy to see me, and I even made friends with a nice group of guys there. That's what kept me going back.

I had questions about what I saw happening at church. People freely expressed themselves when they felt moved by God, raising their hands and sometimes speaking in special languages that it seemed only God could understand. It scared me half to death sometimes, but I never asked Cara about it. I sat back like I did at AA meetings, coolly observing, never participating.

After a few years, my respect for the pastor and the church members had grown enough that I tried not to go to church with a hangover. They treated me well and never talked down to me, and I thought that was the least I could do. On New Year's Eve of 2005, I stopped drinking entirely. I didn't want to jeopardize my truck-driving job by getting a DUI, and sitting around getting drunk wasn't fun anymore. I was a husband, an employee and a father of four. It was time to move on.

In 2007, the pastor of Trinity Full Gospel talked about marriage during his sermon. He described how the Bible defined the role of a husband and father. I knew I wasn't the best, especially after I'd been unfaithful, but since then I thought I'd been pretty good.

However, according to the Bible, I hadn't.

I'd been neglecting Cara for years and years, in our friendship and in the bedroom. I listened to the pastor tell stories about his own marriage and talk about how much he loved his wife. I wasn't as good a husband as I thought. All I'd been doing was providing a roof over Cara and the kids' heads.

If I don't do something, Cara's going to leave.

I needed some outside confirmation of the pastor's standards, so I took one of my cars over to my dad's house so that I could talk to him while we worked on it together. I told him a little about my own situation and the pastor's words.

"Dad, I've just lost my sex drive." That's the best explanation I had.

He raised his eyebrows. "She's young, Dave. You need to straighten up, because she's not going to hang around forever."

New BEGINNINGS

That was the reassurance I needed. The pastor was right.

❧❧❧

First, I needed to learn more about God. I'd had no experience with church growing up.

Cara taught a Sunday school class for children, and I often sat in the classroom to help her by making copies or anything else she needed. At the same time, I listened to what she taught. I learned the stories of the Old Testament and about Jesus and how he loves people and wants to forgive them for the wrong things they've done. As my foundation in Bible knowledge grew, the pastor's teachings began to make sense.

Two years into my elementary Bible education, the chains of guilt and shame that had bound my inner life began to loosen a little. When I drove my truck, I could picture the scene in my mind. I was raising my hands as a worship song played in church on Sunday, my eyes closed and my face turned upward toward God and heaven. Then I was kneeling at the altar in the front of the church, praying with the pastor.

There's nothing holding me back, I'd tell myself. *This Sunday is going to be different.*

The reality, though, wasn't so easy.

I started to stand up and clap when the church congregation sang worship songs, but I couldn't raise my hands to God like the other people. When the pastor

SPEECHLESS

invited people to walk to the front of the church at the end of the sermon and pray, I felt an urge to go up. My rear end, however, seemed glued to the seat, and my knuckles turned white from gripping the edge of the pew.

You're not worthy of going up there, something inside me whispered. *You'll look foolish.* I couldn't will myself to stand up.

We had a special guest speaker one week. Sandi Burris, a woman who travels around the country visiting churches to talk about God's love, spoke at our church for three nights in a row. The first two nights, I followed my pattern: Something moved in my soul. I longed to go to the front of the church. I stayed stuck to my seat.

On the third night, I asked God to help me.

As the music swelled through the church, I stood up and sang louder than I'd ever sung before, no longer self-conscious about my terrible voice. My hands flew into the air, reaching toward God. No longer afraid, I walked down the aisle between the seats at the end of the service. I relished the feeling of the hands of the pastor and my friends from church resting on my shoulders as they prayed for me, asking God to be in control of my life and to forgive me for the bad things I'd done. I slumped as the guilt and shame dissolved, leaving me with a delicious feeling of peace.

☙☙☙

New BEGINNINGS

Cara and I officially became members of Trinity Full Gospel Church in 2012. I joined a class for new converts, but soon the teacher left to lead another church. I was happy for him but sad that I couldn't finish the class.

"Hey, when are you going to find someone to fill in for that class?" I asked the pastor. "I'd really like to finish it."

He looked at me for a moment. "How about you?"

"What about me?"

"Well, what do you think about teaching it?"

I looked at him, dumbfounded. "Are you kidding me?"

"No." The pastor was serious. "I've been watching you the past few years, and I've seen your growth as you've learned more about God. I think you can do it."

"I don't like talking in front of people."

"Neither do I."

Cara and I were getting ready to go on a weeklong vacation, and I told the pastor I would talk to God about the opportunity and give him my answer when I got back.

I said yes. I sweated bullets when each of my 13-week sessions started, but when I settled down and got to know the people in my class, I thoroughly enjoyed it. God had filled me with a soft heart, a new kindness and love for other people that I couldn't wait to share. I'd always been happy to help people I knew, but I'd become eager to volunteer to help anyone I could.

☙☙☙

SPEECHLESS

As part of my role on the church's missions committee, I was asked to travel to a Navajo reservation in New Mexico in 2013 with a group from Trinity Full Gospel Church. Cara had recently switched jobs and couldn't get the time off, so I went without her.

The Navajo people astounded me. They were poor, and many were alcoholics and homeless. They had little education or opportunities for decent work. They didn't have in-depth knowledge of the Bible. But they were happy. They didn't make excuses for themselves. They appreciated all of the work we did helping them repair and fix up their houses.

One night we crowded about 50 people into the simple church building on the reservation. The room only had a simple pulpit in the front, and the walls were water-stained from where the roof leaked. Children ran around. People trickled into the building, filling up the room.

A guitar and drummer played music. The Navajo people lifted their hands, singing with voices loud enough to fill a much larger building. Children waved flags on the stage.

It came so easily and naturally to them. *Do you know how many years I struggled to reach that point?*

I considered in awe how God had changed my life. He took a drunk, angry guy and turned him into a Sunday school teacher who never missed an opportunity to be at church. Just like the Navajo people I met, I didn't have to have my life together to be friends with God. I just had to ask God to open my heart to loving him.

New BEGINNINGS

When I thought about how much God had changed me, I was speechless.

That night, I found my voice. I opened my mouth and sang from the depth of my gut. I talked to God out loud. I threw my hands in the air.

I was free.

CONCLUSION

My heart is full. When I became a pastor, my desire was to change the world. My hope was to see people encouraged and the hurting filled with hope. As I read this book, I saw that passion being fulfilled. However, at Trinity Full Gospel, rather than being content with our past victories, we are spurred to believe that many more can occur.

Every time we see another changed life, it increases our awareness that God really loves people and he is actively seeking to change lives. Think about it: How did you get this book? We believe you read this book because God brought it to you seeking to reveal his love to you. Whether you're a man or a woman, a truck driver or a waitress, blue collar or no collar, a parent or a student, we believe God came to save you. He came to save all of us from the hellish pain we've wallowed in and offer real joy and the opportunity to share in real life that will last forever through faith in Jesus Christ.

Do you have honest questions that such radical change is possible? It seems too good to be true, doesn't it? Each of us at Trinity Full Gospel warmly invites you to come and check out our church family. Freely ask questions, examine our statements, see if we're "for real" and, if you choose, journey with us at whatever pace you are comfortable. You will find that we are far from perfect. Our scars and sometimes open wounds are still healing,

New BEGINNINGS

but we just want you to know God is still completing the process of authentic life change in us. We still make mistakes in our journey, like everyone will. Therefore, we acknowledge our continued need for each other's forgiveness and support. We need the love of God just as much as we did the day before we believed in him.

If you are unable to be with us, yet you intuitively sense you would really like to experience such a life change, here are some basic thoughts to consider. If you choose, at the end of this conclusion, you can pray the suggested prayer. If your prayer genuinely comes from your heart, you will experience the beginning stages of authentic life change, similar to those you have read about.

How does this change occur?

Recognize that what you're doing isn't working. Accept the fact that Jesus desires to forgive you for your bad decisions and selfish motives. Realize that without this forgiveness, you will continue a life separated from God and his amazing love. In the Bible, the book of Romans, chapter 6, verse 23 tells us that the result of sin (seeking our way rather than God's way) is death, but the gift that God freely gives is everlasting life found in Jesus Christ.

Believe in your heart that God passionately loves you and wants to give you a new heart. Ezekiel 11:19 reads, "I will give them singleness of heart and put a new spirit within them. I will take away their stony, stubborn heart and give them a tender, responsive heart" (NLT).

CONCLUSION

Believe in your heart that "if you confess with your mouth that Jesus is Lord and believe in your heart that God raised him from the dead, you will be saved" (Romans 10:9 NLT).

Believe in your heart that because Jesus paid for your failure and wrong motives, and because you asked him to forgive you, he has filled your new heart with his life in such a way that he transforms you from the inside out. Second Corinthians 5:17 reads, "When someone becomes a Christian, he becomes a brand new person inside. He is not the same anymore. A new life has begun!"

Why not pray now?

Lord Jesus, if I've learned one thing in my journey, it's that you are God and I am not. My choices have not resulted in the happiness I hoped they would bring. Not only have I experienced pain, I've also caused it. I know I am separated from you, but I want that to change. I am sorry for the choices I've made that have hurt myself, others and denied you. I believe your death paid for my sins, and you are now alive to change me from the inside out. Would you please do that now? I ask you to come and live in me so that I can sense you are here with me. Thank you for hearing and changing me. Now please help me know when you are talking to me, so I can cooperate with your efforts to change me. Amen.

New BEGINNINGS

Zanesville's unfolding story of God's love is still being written ... and your name is in it. I hope to see you this Sunday!

Bishop T.L. Rowland
Pastor, Trinity Full Gospel

We would love for you to join us at Trinity Full Gospel!

We meet Sunday mornings at 10:30 a.m. at 535 Munson Avenue, Zanesville, OH 43701.

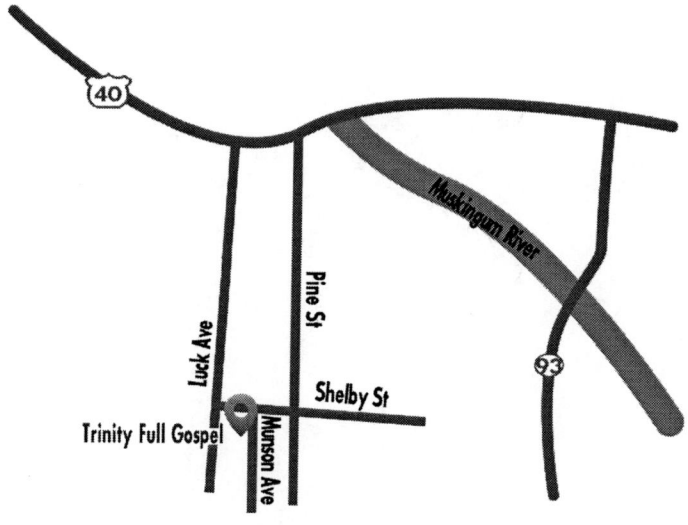

Please call us at 740.452.8478 for directions, or contact us at www.tfgchurch.com.

GOOD CATCH PUBLISHING

For more information on reaching your city with stories from your church, go to
www.testimonybooks.com.

EXPANDED VERSION

Grief☀Share®
Survival Guide

Navigating the Holidays After Loss

Surviving the Holidays

© MMVII, MMXV, MMXXIII, MMXXIV by Church Initiative.

First printing of edition 4.1, June MMXXV.

No part of this book may be reproduced or transmitted in any form or by any means—including electronic, mechanical, photocopy, and recording—or by any information storage or retrieval system, without the written permission of the publisher.

All Scripture quotations, unless otherwise indicated, are taken from the Holy Bible, New International Version®, NIV®. Copyright ©1973, 1978, 1984, 2011 by Biblica, Inc.™ Used by permission of Zondervan. All rights reserved worldwide. www.zondervan.com The "NIV" and "New International Version" are trademarks registered in the United States Patent and Trademark Office by Biblica, Inc.™

Scripture quotations marked (NLT) are taken from the Holy Bible, New Living Translation, copyright ©1996, 2004, 2015 by Tyndale House Foundation. Used by permission of Tyndale House Publishers, Carol Stream, Illinois 60188. All rights reserved.

Contact
Church Initiative
PO Box 1739
Wake Forest, NC 27588-1739

Phone: 800-395-5755 (US and Canada); 919-562-2112 (local and international)
Email: **info@griefshare.org**
Web: **griefshare.org**

Church Initiative: Providing help for people who are hurting
Church Initiative is the parent ministry of GriefShare, a grief recovery support group ministry found in thousands of churches around the world. Our mission is to offer comfort and care to people hurting from life crises, such as grief and divorce. We do that by providing resources that help you navigate the pain and find healing. Programs include Surviving the Holidays (griefshare.org/holidays), a 2-hour event for people grieving a loss; GriefShare, a 13-week support group program; Loss of a Spouse, a short seminar for people who are widowed; and DivorceCare, a 13-week group for people hurting from the pain of a marriage breakup. To learn more, use the contact information above, or see the list of healing resources at the end of this guide.

Welcome

The holidays are quickly approaching. And while their arrival may have been a source of joy in years past, you know the holidays won't be the same without your loved one. If thinking about the impending season is causing snowballing worry, take a breath, you're in the right place. This survival guide is here to help.

In this book, you'll find direction, tips, understanding, and encouragement from grief recovery professionals, and from people who have experienced a loved one's death, to help you navigate the season's challenges.

As you use this guide, I hope it helps you see that you're not alone. Other people have made it through the holidays after loss—and even experienced joy—and you can too. You'll learn some of their stories in the coming pages, and you'll also find a safe place to express your thoughts and feelings in the holiday journal and exercise sections.

While this guide is here as your companion through the holidays, the help doesn't stop there. You can find more grief support by visiting griefshare.org or attending a Surviving the Holidays event (griefshare.org/holidays).

As you navigate this season in grief, I pray that you will feel God's love and comfort with every step you take this holiday season and beyond.

In His love,

Sam Hodges
GriefShare president

Grief is a journey.
Receive continued support along the way.

NEW GROUPS ARE FORMING SOON—BOTH IN PERSON AND ONLINE!

As you travel the path of grief, it's important to have continued support and guidance. People have said that attending GriefShare was the best decision they made for their grief:

"Gave me so many positive coping strategies." – SANDRA

"A tremendous help for my pain." – ROMONA

"GriefShare taught me how to grieve." – CARL

Find your group today!
GRIEFSHARE.ORG/FINDAGROUP

Grief Share

Contents

Intro
How to Use This Guide … vii
Is My Grief Normal? Is It Healthy?: 6 Signs of Healing … viii
If You Feel Suicidal … x

Holiday Survival: Help for the Season … 1
    Chapter 1 *Dealing with Your Emotions* … 3
    Chapter 2 *Having a Plan* … 19
    Chapter 3 *Handling Social Events* … 39
    Chapter 4 *Surviving Thanksgiving & Christmas Day* … 55

A Different Kind of Gift … 83
Help Is Found in the Church … 86

Surviving the Holidays Event Tools … 89
What to Expect Today … 90
What If I'm Not Sure About God? … 91
Video Outline … 92
Meet the Experts … 94
Meet Those Who Shared Their Stories … 97
Take Inventory … 100

About GriefShare … 101
GriefShare Resources … 102

Not sure about God?

Even if you're unsure how you feel about God, you can find hope and healing in these pages. The honest sharing from people who've experienced grief (both those who clung to God and those whose faith was challenged), the expert counsel, and the practical advice are for everyone.

Helpful advice from grief experts & people who've faced loss

Watch this holiday survival video

To hear from people who understand what you're going through is invaluable. This video is filled with compassionate, practical guidance on how to cope with emotional ambushes, social events, and holiday traditions.

"There's something in the video for everyone."
– Mel Erickson, grief educator

Tools for navigating the holiday season

Each chapter includes the following sections:

Survivor Stories: People share holiday grief experiences to help you know what's normal

The Strength to Survive: Daily readings with tips, encouragement, and signs to watch out for that signal healing

Survival Tips: Practical exercises to anticipate and be prepared for challenging moments

Holiday Journal: A private, guided journaling space to process your thoughts and emotions

---

Are you part of a Surviving the Holidays 2-hour event?

This guide can be used on its own or as part of a Surviving the Holidays seminar. (If you're part of an event, see Surviving the Holidays event tools on pages 89–100.) To find a Surviving the Holidays event near you or online, visit **griefshare.org/holidays**.

6 signs of healing

How to know if you're grieving in a healthy way this season ... and beyond

The holidays, with all the traditions and social events, can trigger emotions that make it feel like you're taking steps backward on your grief journey. This is understandable, and even to be expected.

So how do you know if you're moving through grief in a healthy way—in a way that won't result in even more hurt and struggles? These 6 signs of healing will help you identify areas where you're progressing on your grief journey, both during the holidays and throughout your grief journey.

Accepting
Accepting the reality of your loss means acknowledging that even though you don't want this, you have gone through a major loss that will change your life in significant ways.

Dealing with emotions
This involves learning how to process and manage the powerful emotions you will likely experience.

Adjusting
Adjusting to a world without your loved one involves being able to say, "You're not here with me now, so I have to identify what adjustments in my daily or weekly routine might need to be made."

Addressing questions
Death often brings heavy questions like: "Why did God allow this to happen?" Thinking through such questions ultimately shapes your life moving forward.

Continuing without forgetting
Taking steps forward with your life does not mean forgetting your loved one. Instead it means building on the blessings from that relationship; that's how you can honor your loved one.

Sharing comfort
Comforting others facilitates healing. At first you'll need to focus on yourself, but you'll eventually discover how comforting others helps you heal further.

These signs are not one-time events, and they don't happen in any particular order. Instead, they are processes you should go through (some of them repeatedly!) as you adjust to life without your loved one and begin to heal.

You'll learn more about these 6 signs, and what they might look like in your life, throughout this book.

Thoughts of wanting to escape the pain are normal, and maybe you've thought you can't live without your loved one. If you have considered taking your life—pick up the phone. This is especially important if you have thought about *how* to take your life.

"Anytime you have a pattern of suicidal thinking, let somebody else know," says H. Norman Wright, an expert in crisis counseling and intervention, "because the main problem right now is that the only person you're talking with is yourself, and you're not getting good advice from yourself.

"Fleeting thoughts like this are quite normal, but when it becomes a pattern, then it becomes more serious. Never neglect it; never ignore it. Reach out."

What to do if you feel suicidal:

1. **Call 911 or go to the nearest emergency room.**

2. **Call a friend, family member, doctor, pastor, or counselor** immediately, and tell that person you're feeling suicidal. You should not be alone.

3. **Call the Suicide and Crisis Lifeline: 988**

Holiday *Survival*

Help for the Season

A survival guide offers facts and tips that help you foresee danger and survive in the wild. Likewise, this Survival Guide will help you anticipate and find the safest path through any emotional jungles you may find yourself in during the holiday season.

This book is meant to be your companion guide for the days ahead, so read the encouraging words, take notes, and complete the exercises to navigate the holidays with a measure of peace and assurance.

You're not alone.

At a GriefShare group, people understand what you're going through.

Many groups are starting in the new year.
Join one today!

GRIEFSHARE.ORG
Groups meet both in person and online.

Chapter 1

Dealing with Your Emotions

You're shopping for gifts when a familiar Christmas song plays overhead. *Not this song*, you think, as your eyes begin to fill with tears. Hearing your loved one's favorite Christmas song reminds you that this person isn't here to celebrate with you. *How will I ever make it to January?* you wonder.

In this chapter you'll find out:

- **What's normal in holiday grief**
- **How to deal with your emotions**
- **Dangers of numbing the pain**
- **How to avoid emotional ambushes**
- **Why writing a grief letter can help**

Survivor Stories

Often in grief it seems like no one truly understands what you're going through. In the "Survivor Stories" sections in this book, you'll meet people who share their struggles during the holidays.

"The things that were so simple before are hard now. It's hard putting up stockings where it used to be three, and now it's two. It's hard putting up decorations. It's hard going shopping when I don't want to be there. I don't care about the gifts. If I could give up everything and not ever get a gift again to have my mom back, I would."

Shay

"It would have been our daughter Elena's first Christmas with us. She was only with us for eight short months—never got to even celebrate a birthday, let alone Christmas. It felt empty, just felt so surreal."

Robert Rogers, author

The Strength to *Survive*
Daily Readings

These short articles will help you know what to expect over the holidays and offer encouragement and support.

When you'd rather skip the holidays

"The first Thanksgiving, I was more concerned with just getting through the day," shares Carol, whose husband died.

"Christmas," says Willie, "was a day that I really wanted to come—and go. I was glad to be at work because that meant the day went by quicker."

Lois Rabey, author, shares: "I used to feel that I'd like to go to sleep the day before Thanksgiving and wake up January 2nd."

It's hard enough to get up and make it through a day when you've lost a loved one. But when holiday expectations are added on top of that, feelings of loneliness, anxiety, and depression can compound your sadness.

These suggestions will help:

- **Recognize** the holidays will be tough—emotionally, relationally, physically, and spiritually. That's the nature of grief.
- **Don't ignore or numb** difficult emotions. Accept them as part of your grief journey.
- **Set realistic expectations** for yourself, and respect your limitations.
- **Pray** and ask God to help you.

"But you, God, see the trouble of the afflicted; you consider their grief and take it in hand. ... You are the helper of the fatherless." (Psalm 10:14)

God, You see and understand what I'm going through. Please give me strength and help me feel Your comfort this season.

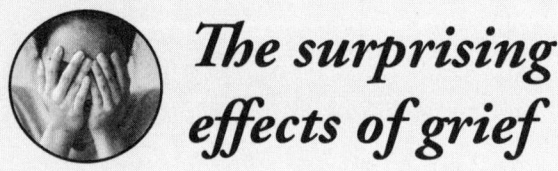

The surprising effects of grief

You're out running errands, but you forget where you're going. You're supposed to bring a Thanksgiving side dish but are too tired to cook. The Christmas songs, movies, and family gatherings are making your throat tighten and your heart race.

Forgetfulness. Exhaustion. Emotional ambushes. Physical problems. You knew the holidays wouldn't be the same, but you probably didn't expect the traditions and events to stir your grief in such complex ways.

Author Randy Alcorn, whose wife died, shares how emotions can feel unpredictable right now: "I would find myself suddenly crying, not for a particular reason. I was generally in a state that I could easily begin to weep."

Chad Bird, author and speaker, describes feeling lost in a haze after his son died: "It's like there was a fog. And I recall just this swirl of emotions, like you're running through a gauntlet, and every step you take, there's another emotion coming along that's striking out at you."

The holidays can also leave you feeling drained, recalls Maria, after the loss of her mom: "I was physically tired. I wasn't sleeping well. I wasn't taking care of myself. I wasn't exercising. I'm a very routine-based person, and I was just kind of floundering."

Grief's effects: Both normal and temporary

It's important to know that the way grief affects you is temporary. The mental, emotional, and physical symptoms you're experiencing can feel disorienting, but just like a fog will eventually lift, so too will the confusing and unpredictable effects of grief. Be patient with yourself and remember that this is the nature of grief.

"How long must I wrestle with my thoughts and day after day have sorrow in my heart?" (Psalm 13:2a)

God, help me to understand that what I'm experiencing is normal and not to place unrealistic expectations on myself.

Is my holiday grief normal?

Living in a world where loss is inevitable means that grief is unavoidable. But you might be surprised by how grief is affecting you. This chart describes common grief reactions and potential problems.

	Common reaction:	**What could be a problem:**
Sadness	• Little desire to celebrate holidays • Crying • Profound awareness of your loved one's absence	• No breaks in sadness (no happy memories to break the tension) • Avoiding people for days • Apathy ("I don't care about anything")
Anger	• Upset that your loved one isn't here for the holidays • Annoyed with insensitive people	• Thoughts of harming yourself/others • So irritable with people that they don't stop by
Worry/ Anxiety	• Jittery or on edge • Dreading holidays or a new year alone • Anxious about not meeting people's expectations	• Panic attacks • Can't turn off "what ifs," making you feel helpless to cope • Avoiding people for days
Guilt	• Feeling bad about celebrating • Feeling like you're letting people down	• Fixating on negative thoughts about yourself • Closing yourself off from others' help
Mental fog	• Forgetting holiday invitations • Difficulty making decisions • Occasionally forgetting commitments	• Relational conflicts • Overcommitting yourself • Bills, appointments, etc., completely ignored

Normal grief reactions gradually fade away over several months. However, if yours linger or get worse, talk to a pastor, physician, or Christian counselor.

Chapter 1: Dealing with Your Emotions

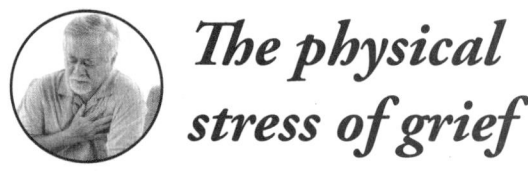

The physical stress of grief

Running out of breath and feeling exhausted are to be expected when you're training for a marathon, but you probably didn't anticipate feeling this worn out during the holidays. If you're experiencing difficult physical symptoms this season, rest assured it's normal.

"Grief is a form of stress," explains trauma surgeon Dr. Kathryn Butler. And when grief is combined with external stressors like holiday expectations, stress hormones remain elevated in the body. "As a result, it is perfectly normal for you to suffer from muscle tension, headaches, and to feel exhausted and depleted all the time."

While these physical responses are normal, they will eventually resolve as you continue to heal. In the meantime, it's important to take care of your body.

Self-care tips to help you feel better:

- Try to get **proper nutrition**. Be sure to drink enough water.*
- Try to get **enough sleep** (8 hours per night). In addition, lie down 2–3 times a day for 20–30 minutes, even if you don't sleep.
- Try to take a **10- to 20-minute walk** each day, depending on your level of fitness. You might try other types of exercise: biking, swimming, pickleball, etc.
- **Set reminders** to take prescription medications.
- For new pains or symptoms, make an **appointment with your physician**.

"Be merciful to me, LORD, for I am in distress; my eyes grow weak with sorrow, my soul and body with grief." (Psalm 31:9)

God, help me keep up my strength so I don't fall apart as I grieve. Grant me the rest and the wisdom I need to make healthy choices for my mind and body.

---

* For guidelines on how much water you should drink daily, search the Mayo Clinic's website: mayoclinic.org.

Beware of numbing the pain

Your grief can be intense this time of year, and it's natural to want relief from the discomfort. However, it's important to avoid unhelpful behaviors that only distract you from the pain temporarily.

Check off the unhelpful behaviors that might tempt you this season:
- ○ Alcohol/drugs
- ○ Overeating
- ○ Getting lost in social media/internet/TV
- ○ Overspending on holiday gifts
- ○ Sex
- ○ Workaholism

The holidays can bring many opportunities to numb your pain, which won't help you. In fact, you're likely to create even more complications.

How to avoid these behaviors
1. ***Check in with yourself.*** For two weeks, every time you are tempted toward an unhelpful response to grief, ask yourself the following:
   - What thoughts and feelings are troubling me? (Be specific.)
   - What numbing and distracting behaviors am I tempted to engage in?
   - What are the pros and cons of giving in to these behaviors?
   - What productive behaviors could replace the unhelpful behaviors?
2. ***Use your answers to start a conversation.*** Talk with a pastor, physician, or other appropriate professional about your answers.

"But as for me, my feet had almost slipped; I had nearly lost my foothold." (Psalm 73:2)

Lord, give me the strength to resist unhealthy temptations. Guide me to other people who can help me find better ways of dealing with my pain.

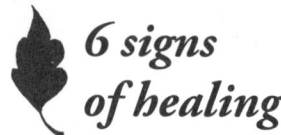

6 signs of healing

Dealing with Emotions
Working through your emotions is a sign of healing (see pp. viii–ix).

The messages of your emotions

Unfortunately, the holidays will look different this year, and you'll struggle with unwanted emotions. But your emotions give you clues about what's important to you. And thinking through them can give you something productive to do about them. Consider this chart:

Maybe you feel	Because …	Productive action
Anger	Friends and family … • Pressure you to attend holiday events • Have too-high expectations of you to get in the holiday spirit • Make insensitive comments	Think of a specific thing you're angry with someone about. Ask yourself, *What constructive action could I take to change this?*
Sadness	You don't want to celebrate without your loved one.	Your loved one can still be part of the holidays. Find ways to honor that person's memory. (For ideas, see pp. 34, 75–76.)
Guilt	You don't feel right about … • Putting up decorations • Going to a party • Laughing • Enjoying the holidays without your loved one	Guilt reveals that you think you did something wrong. Consider: Would your loved one think this? Would God? What could you do to remember how your loved one made the holidays special for you?

You could use this approach to respond to any other emotions you're experiencing as well.

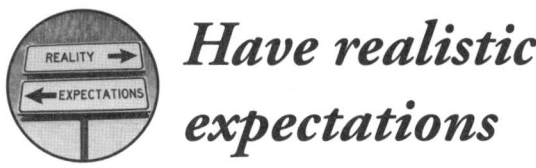

Have realistic expectations

Imagine that you're expecting to have a peaceful, relaxing dinner at a restaurant, but instead a loud, boisterous crowd ends up sitting right behind you. Because your expectations were broken, you're likely to feel irritated and let down. However, if you had known to expect that kind of crowd, you would have been emotionally prepared for the atmosphere (or chosen a different place to eat).

In the same way, it's important to think through your expectations before facing events and traditions this season—*because your expectations will fuel your emotional reactions.*

Consider how your emotions might be different

As you think about upcoming activities, here are ways to prepare yourself:

- Acknowledge that you're likely to feel many conflicting emotions, sometimes all at once
- Understand you probably won't be as joyful as others, and that's okay
- Think about how you *expect* to feel during a coming activity and why it's reasonable to feel that way (not how you *wish* you'd feel)

By setting these expectations beforehand, you can be better prepared and even create an action plan for how to handle these emotions. For example, if you know you'll likely become emotionally overwhelmed during your next family gathering, you can talk to the hosts about a prearranged place to excuse yourself to in order to be alone for a short time, as needed.

"Even in laughter the heart may ache, and rejoicing may end in grief." (Proverbs 14:13)

Heavenly Father, please give me the wisdom to set realistic expectations for myself this season, and to feel prepared for the emotions that will arise.

Reflect

- What expectations do you have for upcoming events and traditions?
- Do you think these expectations are realistic? Why or why not?

Prepared for emotional ambushes

As I was walking around the store, the tears and the memories just started to flow," says Scott, whose wife died from cancer.

Clarissa Moll, podcaster and author whose husband died, shares, "Just when I think all is well—that's when the grief shows up. And I am overwhelmed with the fact he's gone, and I begin to cry."

When you are ambushed by strong emotions, H. Norman Wright, grief and trauma specialist whose wife and son died, offers this reassurance:

> Tears come at some of the most inopportune times. You could be at a holiday gathering or in a store, and all of a sudden the tears come. Best thing is, let them come, and don't apologize. Take charge of it and say, "I'm crying because I've experienced a devastating loss." That's all you have to say. You're alright. You don't need to be fixed.

Expect emotional ambushes. It won't stop them, but that expectation will help lessen the surprise factor.

God offers a place to go where you can find peace and rest: "Jesus said, 'Come to me, all of you who are weary and carry heavy burdens, and I will give you rest. … Let me teach you … and you will find rest for your souls.'" (Matthew 11:28–29b NLT)

God, I'm worn out from my tears, from the constant emotional overload. I am turning to You because my load is too much to bear alone. Give me the strength and rest I need.

Help for loneliness

The holidays heighten feelings of loneliness. "The overwhelming feeling I had my first holiday season was feeling very much alone," shares Mardie, whose husband died. "I didn't feel I was connected to anything or anybody."

"I remember when the calls stopped coming, I just felt so lonely," says Vaneetha, whose infant son died. "I didn't even know what I needed from people." Eventually she concluded, "What I really needed was God. It's easy to forget that the source of strength and comfort is never going to be other people, ultimately. It's always going to be God."

Dr. Elias Moitinho, counselor, reminds us: "Being with people will help you deal with your loneliness. But we need to think in terms of the most important relationship we can ever have—a relationship with God." When you don't have friends and family around this holiday season, God is there.

Not feeling connected to people after losing a loved one is common. But it's important not to cut yourself off from other people. God has given us other people to comfort and care for us during our toughest times. We understand it can be difficult to deal with other people and their lack of understanding and occasional insensitivity. You'll find helpful guidance on interacting with people this season in chapter 3.

"God is our refuge and strength, an ever-present help in trouble. Therefore we will not fear, though the earth give way and the mountains fall into the heart of the sea. ... The LORD Almighty is with us; the God of Jacob is our fortress." (Psalm 46:1–2, 7)

God, You are the only one who truly knows the loneliness I struggle with. It feels like a hollow in my gut that often threatens to consume me. You are the only one who can remedy that. Please fill that emptiness.

Reflect
- When are you loneliest?
- How do you relate to today's passage from Psalm 46?

Survival Tips

The exercises in this section will help you apply the practical ideas in this book to your own life.

Avoid being blindsided

Emotional ambushes are triggered by activities, traditions, songs, sights, sounds, etc., that remind you of past times with your loved one. Mentally preparing yourself will help lessen the ambush factor.

Author Dr. Robert DeVries, whose first wife died, suggests that before you attend a holiday event, replay in your mind the traditions that always involved your loved one. For instance, "If your father [who died] always cut the turkey, think about who's going to do that. Or if your aunt always came with a banana cream pie, somebody bringing a banana cream pie may trigger an emotion."

Answer the following questions to help you prepare.

Holiday preparations: Your loved one likely had a certain role in decorating for the holidays, cooking/baking, gift-giving, etc. How will holiday preparations look different this year?

Holiday get-togethers: How has your loved one's death affected who you'll be getting together with this holiday, compared to past holidays? (Will you miss seeing certain people; is there potential for awkwardness or discomfort; is there a possibility of conflict; etc.?)

 Thanksgiving/Christmas Day: What will you miss most about your loved one's presence on Thanksgiving/Christmas Day?

Write a grief letter

Over the holidays, everyone wants to know how you are doing. The questions can wear you out, as you repeat the same emotionally draining responses. People are full of advice and want to cheer you up: "You should do this! … Go here. … Take part in that."

H. Norman Wright, grief and trauma specialist, suggests you write a grief letter before the holiday season (or prior to specific events). Send it to family and friends, or carry copies to pass out to people as needed.

How to write a grief letter:

- Briefly describe your experience and your feelings.
- Let people know what they can expect from you.
- Tell them what they can do and say that you'd find comforting, and share what's *not* comforting.
- List specific, practical needs they can help with.
- Pass it out by hand, mail, email, social media, or even on your voicemail greeting.

Your emotions will be unique to you, but here's an idea of what to write:

Friends and family,

As you know, I'm going into this holiday without _____. I don't want to ruin the holidays for everyone else, but to be honest, I have no holiday cheer. I'll probably have to excuse myself early from events or go off alone in another room. I don't feel like talking much.

I might cry—perhaps in the middle of your party. My tears are part of my healing, so don't be embarrassed by them. Pat my shoulder and give me a brief hug to let me know you're there. Words are not necessary.

Please talk about _____. It would hurt me so much if you avoid speaking _____'s name. I like to hear stories and memories about him/her.

My energy level is going to be low this season. I can't do everything I used to do. If someone could help me with some home and holiday tasks, that would be appreciated. Specifically, I need help to put up and take down my tree. I could use help with housework too (I can't seem to keep up with it).

Thank you for caring about me and praying for me. Your love and concern are a comfort.

Holiday Journal

What to do with your holiday emotions

Journaling can help you slow down your thoughts and sort through the tangled emotions you're experiencing this Thanksgiving and Christmas season, providing some peace of mind.

Use a separate notebook or journal to write your responses to one (or more) of the topics below. This is for your eyes only, so don't worry about spelling, being neat, or guarding your words.

- Psalm 147:3 says that the Lord heals the brokenhearted and binds up their wounds. Tell Him in what ways your heart is broken this season, and ask Him to bind up your wounds.

- Read the comment below and share your personal thoughts about crying or showing emotions in public.

    > "Emotions are natural for all of us, and yes, other people may become uncomfortable with them. The Bible is filled with examples of people weeping in public. Crying is not shameful at all. A good show of emotion from time to time, even at a party, shows authenticity for the significant loss you've experienced in your life." Dr. Robert DeVries, author whose wife died

- Make a list of the emotions you've been dealing with recently. For each one, write down: What memories, beliefs, or desires are associated with this emotion? Regarding any desires you jot down, are there ways to satisfy them in a healthy way? (Breaking this up into multiple sittings can be helpful.)

Chapter 2

Having a Plan

When baking bread, following a recipe helps ensure that the bread will hold together. If the recipe isn't followed, who knows how the bread will turn out? In the same way, creating a flexible holiday plan will help you know what to expect and give you a degree of control this season.

This chapter discusses:

- **Whether or not to continue holiday traditions that are so hard without your loved one**
- **Why having a plan is crucial**
- **How to create a straightforward, yet flexible, plan**
- **How to take care of yourself and your children this season**

Survivor Stories

Having a plan in place—one you hold loosely—can help you face social events. Read how Cindy and Bekah handled holiday get-togethers.

"As I approached the first Thanksgiving, I put a plan in place, but I held it loosely. It was helpful to have a planned answer ready for when people would ask, 'How are you?' I might say, 'I have good days and bad days. Today is a good day'—so I could be honest and authentic about my feelings without making them uncomfortable."

Cindy Bultema, author

"The first year after Rob died, I avoided invitations. I said no to almost everything. But I'll admit that when I said no, I was worried that they'd never ask again."

Bekah

The Strength to *Survive*
Daily Readings

Find ways to reduce stress and create a meaningful, doable, flexible plan suited to you.

The importance of having a plan

"Winging it is a poor choice if you're dealing with the holidays. Often it comes from, *I don't want to think about it or deal with it*. But not thinking about it doesn't mean the holidays are going to disappear," says Dr. Susan Zonnebelt-Smeenge, whose husband died.

This season you will be faced with memories, traditions, expectations, and responsibilities. Having a plan keeps you from becoming overwhelmed. Author Dr. Robert DeVries, whose wife died of cancer, shares:

- **Planning** simply means you decide what and how much you want to do.
- **Prioritizing** means if there are 15 holiday activities you might be involved in, you choose 1 or 2 that are most important to you.

Whatever you plan, be flexible in allowing yourself to adjust it. And you don't have to make a plan on your own! Ask someone to help you. If you have children, involve them in the planning process; this will also aid their healing. The charts and tips in this chapter can guide you.

"Commit to the LORD whatever you do, and he will establish your plans." (Isaiah 41:10)

God, please help me to create a plan during the holidays and stay flexible. And help me feel Your presence as I navigate this new season.

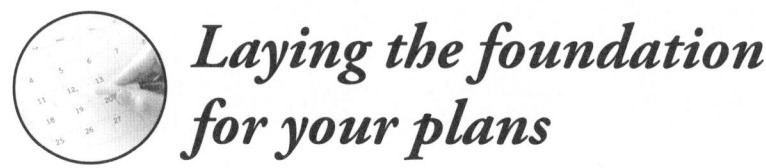# *Laying the foundation for your plans*

As you make decisions about what activities to participate in, who to spend time with, and how to handle unexpected situations, you'll want to lay the right foundation for your plans. Dr. Paul David Tripp, counselor, offers three tips:

1. **Know yourself.** Know your strengths and weaknesses. Make plans that focus on your strengths, and be cautious about those that bring out your weaknesses. For instance, if spending time with grandkids brings you joy, plan a visit. If at the office party you might be tempted to numb yourself with alcohol—don't go. Put things on the calendar that will refresh your spirit: Lunch with a friend? A hike alone with God? A special church concert?

2. **Consider who's best for you.** You have a good idea of what type of advice or support your friends and family will offer you. Plan to spend time with those who will listen to you, lift you up, and encourage you in your faith. Avoid those who will rush you in your grief or pressure you to lower your moral standards.

3. **Commit to reading and studying your Bible** to learn more about who God is and what He promises. As you dive into His Word, you'll find peace and reassurance for life's uncertainties. How do the verses below help ease any worries you have as you anticipate and plan for the coming holidays?

"The LORD comforts his people and will have compassion on his afflicted ones." (Isaiah 49:13b)

"Ah, Sovereign LORD, you have made the heavens and the earth by your great power and outstretched arm. Nothing is too hard for you." (Jeremiah 32:17)

"For the LORD is good and his love endures forever; his faithfulness continues through all generations." (Psalm 100:5)

God, You know me better than anyone, and You have promised to be with me in all situations. Help me to be prepared for the days ahead.

Planning vs. controlling

"Perfect plans cannot ultimately protect you from anything," explains counselor Susan Lutz. "This is a broken world. God doesn't want you to put your hope in nothing going wrong. He says, 'I want you to put your hope in the fact that I will never leave you or forsake you, even when things are going wrong. I will walk you through it.'"

Having a good plan is wise and will help you move forward in healing, but trying to create and adhere to "the perfect plan" is neither wise nor biblical! As you know, things happen every day that can change your best-laid plans in an instant.

"Planning is a good thing," but keep in mind, says counselor Dr. Paul David Tripp, "there's a crucial difference between planning and control. We plan what we think is best for situations over which we have no [complete] control. It's right to plan, but part of planning is humility and flexibility.

"Planning is looking ahead, trying to anticipate problems and solve them before you get there. That's a responsible thing to do, but we're never going to be sovereign.

"So you've got to hold your plan with an open hand because you're never in control of the people and situations of your life. Our hope is not in *our* control, but in *God's* faithfulness."

Planning with humility and flexibility under God's guidance becomes a tool of healing.

"Many are the plans in a man's heart, but it is the LORD's purpose that prevails." (Proverbs 19:21)

Dear God, I need Your help. You alone have the perfect plan for all people and all situations, so I'd best be discussing this with You! Help me to be flexible with my plans and understand it's okay if things work out differently than I expected.

Simplifying your plans

You can't do it all this holiday season. Whatever you think you must do, consider how you could simplify the things that seem overwhelming or that may be a financial burden. The key is to look for a balance between meaningful and manageable. (See the Survival Tips at the end of this chapter to help you put your plan on paper.)

To simplify this year, you could:

Be selective about decorating: Instead of putting up every decoration, consider which are most important to you (and fit your current energy level). If you choose to have a tree, you could skip hanging your typical ornaments and decorate the tree with small stuffed animals, mementos, or items from nature. Or consider a tabletop tree or a centerpiece that focuses on the true meaning of Christmas.

Realize you don't need to purchase a gift for everyone: If finances are tight, consider a personal message in a card; a gift of a meal, dessert, or time; or a bag filled with that person's favorite snacks. Be up-front with family and friends about changes in gift-giving.

Consider holiday meal shortcuts: You could have each guest bring a dish to share, order in, go out, have make-your-own turkey sandwiches, or ask someone else to plan this year's meal.

Be sure to call on God for help this season!

> **"Then you will call, and the LORD will answer; you will cry for help, and he will say: Here am I."** (Isaiah 58:9a)

Lord, give me the courage to speak up and let others know I will be celebrating more simply this year and that I'd appreciate their support and understanding.

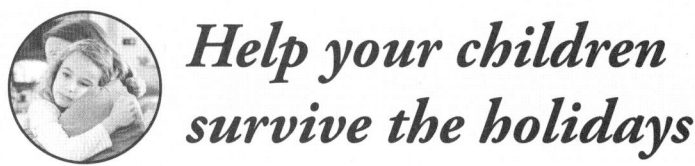

Help your children survive the holidays

Your children might have concerns about the coming holidays. *How are we going to cut down the Christmas tree without Dad? Who is going to make our special Christmas breakfast? If we aren't going to Grandma's for dinner, where will we go?*

They, too, will struggle with sadness, loneliness, and anger. In your holiday planning, think about how you'll prepare your kids for the changes this season and how you'll help them communicate and express their emotions.

Talk with them ahead of time

"Before the season started, I said, 'We're going to do the best we can and celebrate what the season's about, even though Daddy's gone. He would want us to do that. We're going to have some new traditions, and it will be okay. This will feel different. And there may be things you're going to feel sad about. Come talk to me, and we'll work through it with God's help,'" shares author Lois Rabey.

Include them in holiday planning

Ask your kids for their input regarding holiday plans. For instance, if you don't have the energy to put up all the exterior and interior decorations, ask your kids for help in deciding which are most important to you as a family. If the annual gingerbread house decorating is too much, ask the kids for alternate ideas.

Counselor Dr. Paul Tautges recommends you ask your children which past traditions mean the most to them, the ones they'd like to do again this year. "Involving your children in that discussion teaches them that in grief, we all have to take small steps in working through it."

Help them express their emotions

When kids are upset about something, they often don't express their feelings in words. Instead, their anxieties can come out in the form of misbehavior, throwing fits, or unusual quietness and withdrawal.

Dr. Brad Hambrick, counselor, advises, "When our kids are grieving, one of the best things we can do is just be near them, be in the room while they're playing. We're in that shared space, so the thoughts moving through their minds get the opportunity to spill out through their mouths."

You can also open the door of communication by sharing what you're feeling. Then make sure you listen, instead of talk!

"Don't worry about anything; instead, pray about everything. Tell God what you need, and thank him for all he has done. Then you will experience God's peace. … His peace will guard your hearts and minds as you live in Christ Jesus." (Philippians 4:6–7 NLT)

Lord, taking care of my children is so difficult when I'm hurting this badly. Please give me strength to guide my children through healthy grieving. I will entrust my children to You. I pray that they come to have a relationship with You.

Reflect

How will you open the lines of communication with your children (or guide them to another safe adult to share with)?

Children's grief
Videos for parents on how to help a grieving child
GRIEFSHARE.ORG/CHILDREN

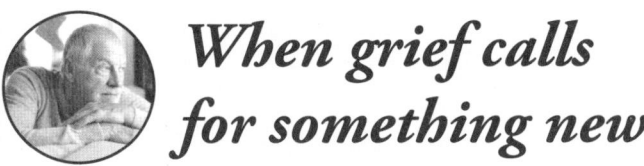

When grief calls for something new

For those of us facing grief, the cheeriness of the holidays and the thought of maintaining traditions can be off-putting and overwhelming. *Do we have to do this? Do we need to go through all the decorating and fuss? Is it unhealthy if I just opt out?* These are fair questions to ask, says counselor Dr. Brad Hambrick.

As you think about past traditions and activities, consider these points:

- **Some traditions were centered on the person you lost**, and repeating those traditions may not make sense anymore.

- **Some were more focused on other people**, maybe other family members, so you might consider whether you have the energy to do them this year.

- **Some traditions seem like they'll just hurt too much right now.**

Making adjustments

It's completely fine to pause a past tradition for a while and slowly bring it back later. Therapist Ron Deal watched this happen after his son's death:

> We "sort of" did Christmas the two years after Connor's death. We gave gifts to the other two boys. We didn't even try to do the tree and ornaments: Those traditions were just too painful. Slowly over time, they began to enter back into the picture in different ways, with new meanings that they didn't have before.
>
> A lot of grief is a "live and learn" experience. For the holidays, try something and if it doesn't work, you know what not to do next year. Each year, keep trying until you find what works for your family. It's not an easy journey, but it is the road you have to walk. It's how you move forward.

Adjusting your traditions can feel off-putting at first, but you can eventually have peace of mind, even amid the grief. As Randy Alcorn, author and former pastor, shares, "Peace is kind of a settled sense of well-being that life is okay. At first, your life isn't going to [feel] okay, but it can become so more and more."

"The LORD gives strength to his people; the LORD blesses his people with peace." (Psalm 29:11)

Lord, please guide me this holiday season to make adjustments as needed and to know Your peace, Your strength, throughout these changes.

Relieving some pressure

You might wonder if it's better to try and keep the holidays the same as much as possible or whether to do something completely different this year. There is no right or wrong answer to this question, as long as you recognize that you cannot duplicate past holidays.

As counselor Susan Lutz explains, "There may be sadness in the fact that a holiday is never going to be the same after a loss. But I think it's better than adopting a crushing burden of trying to re-create something that cannot be re-created."

It's important to prayerfully consider what is best for you and your family this year, and then know that you can reassess next year to determine if you want to do things differently.

"I was putting too much pressure on myself in my desire to make things as normal as possible for my husband and my father-in-law that first Christmas after my mother-in-law died," says Connie.

JoAnne shares, "It really helped me to get away and do Christmas differently than we'd ever done it before. The first year after Jody died, I took a trip to South Florida with my sons. It helped not to have those strong emotional memories in my face. We did that for the next four years."

"Cast your cares on the LORD and he will sustain you." (Psalm 55:22a)

Lord, what would be best for me this holiday season? What plans would be helpful for my healing and still be respectful to my family members? Teach me how to hear Your voice and follow closely after You. You know what's best for me. Thank You for guiding me through Your words in the Bible and through the wise counsel of mature Christian friends.

Reflect

- Which holiday traditions/events do you think you'll try to maintain this year?

- What do you think of JoAnne's idea to go someplace completely different for Christmas?

- How will you put Psalm 55:22 into practice in your holiday decision-making?

Honoring your loved one in new traditions

Your loved one is no longer present to celebrate the holidays with you. Yet, that doesn't necessarily mean he or she has to be absent from this season's celebrations. Here's how some people have honored their deceased loved ones with new traditions.

- **Tree of "favorites":** "What we've decided to do is to make a 'dad tree,' and we decorate it with all sorts of ornaments that relate to the university he went to, his favorite football team, and the things he enjoyed doing, like fishing. We put a baseball cap with his school emblem on the top." – *Sheila*

- **Your loved one's ornaments:** "We have tons of ornaments we've made throughout our lives, and my mom has taken all of Hannah's ornaments and put them in a separate box. The whole family puts Hannah's ornaments on the Christmas tree together." – *Jemma*

- **Lighting candles:** "My children and I light a candle for my [deceased] husband through the whole month of December every night at dinner. I've made a candle for them with a picture of them and their father wrapped around the candle." – *Sheila*

- **Silly gifts to remember:** "My family decided we would come together and have a celebration in honor of my sister-in-law, and we would all open the gifts we had purchased for her. As we opened the gifts, we tried to do an imitation of her and tried to react as she would when she would open the gift. We had such a great time remembering her in a special way. We decided that every year we would buy silly gifts in remembrance of her." – *Sabrina D. Black, counselor*

- **Stocking gift blessings:** "My son's stocking still gets hung over on the mantel, and the gifts that would be given to him are given to somebody else to bless them." – *Ron Deal, marriage and family therapist*

- **Giving to a cause:** "Give gifts to a cause that meant a lot to your loved one." – *Susan Lutz, counselor*

- **Serving those in need:** "One of my friends had a coworker whose church served Thanksgiving dinner to the community, and they needed extra help serving. So we helped serve Thanksgiving dinner. That worked out well." – *Carol*

- **Finding someone who is alone:** "I visited a girlfriend of mine who was single and by herself." – *Lois Rabey, author*

- **Gifts of remembrance:** "I prayed and asked the Lord to help me find a gift for everyone in the family to remember my husband." – *Jeannine*

6 signs of healing

Adjusting
Blending family traditions is a way to adjust to life after loss (see pp. viii–ix).

Blending family traditions

Traditions can make holidays special for children, and traditions can also help adult children adjust after the loss of their parents. After Tom's parents died, his wife, Connie, asked *her* family to consider adopting some of his parents' holiday traditions. Tom says:

> My parents liked to open Christmas gifts one at a time. So each of us would open a gift and then the others would sit back and take it all in. But my wife's family had a different tradition: Everybody ripped into their presents at the same time.
>
> What's been great, since my parents' passing, is that Connie has introduced my family's tradition to her family: "Hey, let's not open all of our gifts all at once, but let's spend time enjoying what other people are receiving."
>
> And then my mom would make a birthday cake for Jesus every year, or have somebody make one for her. That was something I missed dearly. My wife has also introduced that to her family, and it's been great.

Holding on to traditions, for some grievers, becomes a comforting way of honoring the memory of the person who started the traditions years ago. Death always disrupts our lives, but favorite memories can help stabilize us as we look toward the future.

"May your unfailing love be my comfort." (Psalm 119:76a)

Lord, help me to accept what needs to be new this holiday season, and to draw comfort from past traditions we might want to hold on to. Draw us closer together and closer to You.

Continuing
Continuing life while honoring your loved one's memory is a sign of progress (see pp. viii–ix).

Memories of your loved one

Incorporating your loved one's memory in your holiday festivities is one way to celebrate his or her impact on your life. The following are different ways people have chosen to honor their loved one's memory during this season:

- **Character trait tags on the tree:** "One family I knew made tags with character traits written on them and tied them on the Christmas tree. Family members would go to the tree and take a character trait. If it said, 'sense of humor,' they would share a story about Grandpa's sense of humor. If it said 'exaggerator,' they'd share a story of Grandpa exaggerating something," says Mel Erickson, author and grief educator.

- **Loved one's favorite meal:** "My brother was born on December 6th. The tradition in our home was to eat the family member's favorite meal on their birthday," shares Dr. Tate Cockrell, counselor. He and his family continue this tradition by sharing his brother's favorite meal, shepherd's pie, every December 6th.

- **Lighting candles:** "One of the things that we still do is we light a candle, and it stays on as long as somebody's at home. On Christmas I do that, and now it's for my mom, my dad, my son, my husband, and many others who've died. The whole time I'm at home, that candle is lit," shares Karen.

- **Being grateful:** "Mom had a Thanksgiving tradition where we'd write something we were thankful for," says Jason. "That's something we want to continue doing."

- **Stocking stuffed with holiday memories:** "You might use a Christmas stocking as a place where people can put treasured holiday memories, and then have a time of sharing those memories," suggests Mel Erickson.

Living your life now doesn't mean forgetting your loved one. Brainstorm with your family and friends to come up with creative ways to honor the memory of your loved one during the events and traditions this year.

Survival Tips

The exercises in this section will help you apply the practical ideas in this book to your own life.

Be careful not to overburden yourself

"Think about what would make the holidays manageable and meaningful."
Dr. Ramon Presson, family counselor

Your energy is likely to be low this holiday season. It's wise to plan ahead and set careful limits on what you will do this year. But be flexible. What you decide today might change later, and that's okay.

Holiday decorations
Check the items below you'd like to do, those most important to you. And think about how you might do them in a way that won't overburden you (see examples).

- ○ Christmas tree (get a smaller tree, buy a pre-decorated tree, have your grandchildren decorate and take down your tree, enlist help from a friend)

- ○ Interior/exterior lights (only have lights inside this year, ask for help putting up exterior lights, use small electric candles in the windows instead)

- ○ Other decorations: _____

Gift-giving
Check ideas that will help keep gift-giving at a manageable level.

- ○ Buy gift cards to keep it simple.
- ○ Shop early.
- ○ Ask someone to help you shop. Write the name of a person you could ask: _____
- ○ Brainstorm low-cost gift ideas, such as bags of assorted treats or framed photos.
- ○ Consider passing on something special that belonged to your loved one.
- ○ Give a gift to a cause important to your loved one instead of giving presents.
- ○ Cut down on gift-giving this year, and prayerfully consider how to communicate that to family members.

Christmas cards
Check what you might do this year. Send cards only if it is important/meaningful to you.

- ○ Send e-cards.
- ○ Post your card and message on social media.
- ○ Limit the number of cards you send (e.g., only to out-of-town relatives).
- ○ Send a photo card of a beautiful scene, Scripture, or preprinted meaningful message.
- ○ Ask someone to help you with cards. Here's who could help: _____
- ○ Skip sending cards.

Holiday meals & baking

Perhaps in the past you've done the bulk of the holiday meals and baking—and you truly enjoyed it. Or maybe your loved one was the person who spearheaded the holiday cooking.

But this year you may not feel like cooking much at all. If so, don't overburden yourself by preparing extravagant meals. "Our Christmas tradition," shares Jeannine, "was that my husband [who died] would cook breakfast. That first Christmas I bought donuts the night before—because I knew I wouldn't be able to cook breakfast."

Check ideas that might work for you this year.

- ○ Allow someone else to host the Thanksgiving or Christmas meal.
- ○ Have a potluck supper, where no one is responsible for the bulk of the cooking.
- ○ Go out to a restaurant.
- ○ Pre-order a turkey or ham and side dishes.
- ○ Choose not to make things from scratch.
- ○ Enlist cleaning help both before and after meals. Excuse yourself from this, if needed.
- ○ Instead of inviting people for a large meal, plan for desserts and coffee instead.
- ○ Purchase cookies or desserts, or use ready-bake cookies.
- ○ Other ideas: _____

Ask for and accept help

Your family and friends may be looking for ways to come alongside you and lessen your pain. Allow them to support you in concrete ways. Let them do or help with the thing you would like to see done, yet have no energy to do.

Regarding holiday meal responsibilities, ask yourself, *Is this something someone else can do? Or is this something someone might enjoy helping me with?*

Chapter 2: Having a Plan

Holiday Journal

Having a plan

Be sure to plan time for reflection this season, for processing and talking with God about the emotions and stresses of the holidays. Use a separate notebook or journal to reflect on the topics below.

The sights, sounds, and smells of the holiday season will trigger new waves of emotions and memories: Christmas lights in the neighborhood. Carols on the radio. Apple pie in the oven. What holiday sights, sounds, and smells have been an emotional trigger for you? What happened? How did you react?

- Sights:
- Sounds:
- Smells:

Slow down the chaos

Your thoughts and emotions may be on overload this holiday season. A guided journal can help you sort your emotions and find joy.

Discover *Reflections* today:
GRIEFSHARE.ORG/JOURNAL

Chapter 3

Handling Social Events

"Are you coming to the Christmas party?" your friend asks. Your mind starts racing as you think about the insensitive comments and uncomfortable conversations you might have to endure if you go. You want to say no, but you don't want to hurt anyone's feelings or let people down.

This chapter discusses:

- **The difference between solitude and isolation**
- **The importance of being around encouraging people**
- **How to respond to social invitations**
- **How to respond to difficult questions and comments**

Survivor Stories

The first Christmas arrived, and Sabrina and Marion both attended family get-togethers.

"My sister-in-law was this great, fun-loving person, and I remember that first Christmas [after she died] everybody brought a gift for her. We bought fuzzy house shoes and stuffed animals, and we wrapped it all up. But when we brought the gifts to the house, they sat there. We realized she wasn't there to open them, and nobody wanted to open the gifts."

Sabrina D. Black, counselor

"The first Christmas after my husband passed we spent at my daughter's house, and I helped her during the hustle and bustle. But after everybody else was back home, that was the difficult time. That had been the time for my husband and me to simply watch a movie, clean up the leftovers, or reflect on the day. It was saddest at the end of the day."

Marion

The Strength to Survive
Daily Readings

Find guidance on who to spend time with this season and how to handle social events.

Choosing to spend time alone or with others

To heal from your pain, you need a healthy balance of solitude and interaction. This is especially important during the busy holiday season. Ellie shares the difference between solitude and isolation:

"**Solitude** is when you need some time just to be alone with your memories, with your thoughts, and with the Lord. I set aside a portion of each day for that.

"**Isolation** is when you begin to shut people out of your life, staying at home and not going out the front door. Isolation separates you not only from people, but from God."

To experience the benefits of solitude and interaction, it's important to evaluate situations before you're in them. Ask yourself these questions:

If I choose to be with people today, will I:

- Be willing to talk about my loved one and share memories about him or her if opportunities arise?
- Safely express my grief if I am ambushed by difficult emotions?
- Be honest and ask for any needed help?

If I choose to be alone, will I:

- Take time to dwell on my latest feelings and thoughts?
- Talk to God about those feelings, seek His help, and accept His comfort?
- Avoid the temptation to numb my pain?

If you would answer "no" to any of those questions, rethink going into the situation, or take steps to make the experience more beneficial. For instance, if you realize you might not be able to talk about your loved one at an event, write a grief letter to give to those attending.*

If you realize that, when alone, all you'll think about is your sadness and despair, plan to occupy your time with an activity such as (a) prayer, (b) reading a devotional book, or (c) reading a book on healing from grief.

The important thing is thinking before committing to time alone or time with others and setting boundaries.

"[Jesus] went up on a mountainside by himself to pray. ... He was there alone." (Matthew 14:23b)

"Two are better than one. ... If either of them falls down, one can help the other up." (Ecclesiastes 4:9a–10a)

God, I pray that I can find healing through both time alone and time with others.

Reflect

- When you choose to be alone, what do you tend to do?
- What suggestions in this article will you use to move forward with your healing?

* See p. 16 for instructions on writing a grief letter.

6 signs of healing — **Accepting**
Recognizing and accepting changes shows healing, but isolating yourself can get in the way (see p. viii).

A problem with isolating

In this holiday season that emphasizes celebrations and social events, it can feel easier to stay home and avoid potential discomfort. However, counselor Dr. Tate Cockrell reminds us it's dangerous to hibernate through the holidays.

When people isolate, he says, they end up getting more depressed. "They're left to their own negative thoughts. They're not engaging the outside world. They're not investing in anybody outside of themselves. So it doesn't provide what they're hoping for. They're hoping for some level of relief, but ultimately what happens is things get worse."

Now, that doesn't mean you need to accept every invitation or stay as long as everyone else. Just beware of isolating!

Dr. Paul Tautges, counselor, also emphasizes the need for community: "Romans 12 says it's good for us to weep with those who weep and to rejoice with those who rejoice. That's part of the way God has made us. We need other people.

"So intentionally staying in contact and having conversations is an important part of working through grief. Talking with my siblings and my kids about my [deceased] father, and the things they remember most about him, was really helpful to me."

"Rejoice with those who rejoice; mourn with those who mourn."
(Romans 12:15)

God, I know I'll miss my loved one so much this holiday season. Help me reach out to others so that I don't become isolated.

Who should you spend time with this holiday?

Simply being around other people doesn't necessarily help you heal and recover from your pain. What's important is to spend time with the kind of people who will encourage your healing and won't derail it.

Identify safe, uplifting friends

"It's important to identify who are the safe people in your life. Who are the ones who are going to nurture you, to build you up? Not to berate you or say, 'Well, get over it. You know it's been six months now.'"
– *H. Norman Wright, grief and trauma expert*

"When I've had such desperate feelings of loneliness, especially at the holidays, it's been important for me to spend time with other folks who have felt the same way and be told, 'Hang on; it feels like you might not make it, but you are going to make it.'" – *JoAnne, whose husband died*

"You want somebody who's not afraid of suffering, somebody who is ready to walk with you and wait with you as that process continues."
– *Susan Lutz, counselor*

Try seeking help at church

"Church can be one of the places that's the most difficult to go to, but church is also the place you're going to receive the most help and care."
– *Lois Rabey, author*

"It was hard to make it through with no family around, so I made some phone calls and tried to get closer to the people at church; I felt like they were part of my family." – *Bill, whose wife died*

Reflect

- Who are the "safe people" in your life? If you can't think of anyone, how could you find them? (In church, a GriefShare support group)
- What do you think would be the result if you reached out to the safe people in your life instead of isolating?

Tuning in to your "social bandwidth"

As with holiday traditions, there is no single response to holiday invitations that fits every grieving person all the time. For some situations, counselor Dr. Brad Hambrick suggests you think about your own "social bandwidth." Here's how:

Step 1. *Ask yourself:*
- When I go to work or to other casual social events, how do I respond there?
- How settled am I in other social situations?

Step 2. *Consider who might be there:*

"Close friends and family are probably grieving alongside you," says Dr. Hambrick. "They get it. You will be remembering together, and there can be a sweetness to the shared memory. A work party, however, may feel more off-putting and irreverent."

Ultimately, understanding factors like that can help you get a sense of whether it's wise to go this year or hold off and maybe go next year.

There's also a way to expand your social bandwidth, if you choose to accept an invitation. Ron Hutchcraft, author and speaker, says, "Think about looking for opportunities to be an encouragement to somebody at the gathering. Thinking about others is always going to be part of the healing process. Go with the thought of giving."

Lord, please give me wisdom to know how to respond to invitations this year. Help me see which ones could be encouraging to attend and how I might even be an encouragement to others who are there.

# How to respond to invitations

Being put on the spot can make you feel stressed and say things you don't mean, but being prepared can help you feel in control. This is why it's important to think through how you'll respond to invitations this season. These people share helpful suggestions:

With flexibility

"You might say, 'Can you just hold my invitation lightly? I'm planning on coming, but it may change that day.'" – *H. Norman Wright, grief expert*

"My escape plan for events was to drive myself there and be willing to say, 'Hey, I need to leave.' I would inform the host beforehand that 'if all of a sudden I am gone, don't worry. I'm okay.' That helped me have security that if I became overwhelmed, I'd know what to do." – *Mike*

With honesty

"I'm a people pleaser. I'm afraid to say no or disappoint someone. In the past I've made the mistake of going to the Christmas party when I didn't want to. I ended up resenting everything about it or feeling upset that I got pressured into it. Grief has taught me how to speak up for myself."
– *Heather*

"Don't commit to that party just because you want to please someone. Just be honest and say, 'I'm still in the process, some good days, some not so good, so I'll let you know.'" – *Dr. Zoricelis Davila, psychotherapist*

"Be honest with the host and say, 'My grief is a roller coaster. I might start out having a good day, and it deteriorates, or I might start out having a miserable day, and it passes. So is it okay if I don't let you know if I'm coming until the day of the event?'" – *Mel Erickson, grief educator*

With creativity

"I found that making the holiday visit either just before the holiday, or after, made for a much better visit. I didn't have to fight holiday traffic. I was able to have quality time with people and actually have a conversation without noise in the background. It worked much better." – *Mardie*

How to respond to comments & questions

"How are you?" This simple question can quickly lead to anxiety: Do you explain how you're feeling and risk the flood of emotions? Or do you simply say you're fine? These suggestions can prepare you for social events.

Plan your responses

"Have a few things scripted beforehand that you're going to say. Then answer calmly: 'This is where I am' and put a gracious end to the conversation [if desired]. If you don't have things scripted beforehand, you can flounder, and that can make you feel anxious and awkward." – *Omar King, counselor*

"Don't feel like you have to give explanations to people. If you want to respond, you can say something general, 'I'm going through the process,' and then change the subject." – *Dr. Zoricelis Davila, psychotherapist*

"What helps is to be very honest when people ask how you are doing. That's healthy for you, but it's also healthy for other individuals because you are teaching them about the journey of grief that they'll have to go through at some point." – *H. Norman Wright, grief and trauma expert*

Be prepared for insensitivity and show grace

"You need to accept that people don't always know the right thing to say. They're going to say the wrong thing at times. So, be prepared ahead of time for the hurt, and nurture a heart that is ready to forgive." – *Dr. Paul Tautges, counselor*

"When someone would say insensitive things, I would speak words back to myself, 'Sheila, you know they don't understand. Give them grace. Forgive them. They don't know it's hurtful.'" – *Sheila, whose husband died*

Reflect

- What questions are you most worried about receiving?
- If someone says something that hurts or offends you, what do you think it looks like to respond with forgiveness and grace?

"I Don't Want to Bring Others Down"

"I didn't want to put a damper on anyone else's joy. So I put on a happy face and tried to be the sister, the daughter, the aunt, that everybody wanted to see. Putting on that happy face was a heavier burden than I was emotionally able to carry at the time," shares Mardie.

Pretending you are doing fine not only hurts you, but is unfair to those around you. "Other people have different expectations then," says Dr. Susan Zonnebelt-Smeenge, psychologist. "They expect that you're doing well and that you won't need any more from them. You're sabotaging yourself if you aren't honest."

Think about times you've said, "I'm doing okay," when inside you were screaming the opposite. Being honest about your pain is a large part of moving forward through grief because it sets the expectation for everyone around you by showing them that it's okay to talk about your lost loved one; it's okay to cry during a party or celebratory event; and it's okay to be sad when other people around you are happy.

Marilyn shares how she approaches social situations with honesty since her husband's death: "I do get the question, how are you doing? And I say, 'I'm doing okay. I'm hurting. I have a hole in my heart, but I'm getting better.'"

Although being honest with people is valuable, that doesn't mean you need to share everything with everyone. Briefer comments will be better with some people. Discretion is always important.

"Therefore each of you must put off falsehood and speak truthfully to your neighbor." (Ephesians 4:25a)

Lord, help me to be honest with myself and with other people. Give me the humility to accept help, support, and prayers from others.

Reflect

Name the people you typically pretend around, saying "I'm okay" when you're not. What holds you back from being honest around those people?

Survival Tips

The exercises in this section will help you apply the practical ideas in this book to your own life.

What to say when ...

You're invited to a party. You plan to attend, but have misgivings. People's questions and comments can be exhausting: "You just have to come." "How are you doing?" "You're not yourself. Let go of your sadness for a little bit and just enjoy the party." ...

Use the following responses to help communicate with the host before you attend and with people at the party. Tip: Send the responses to people in advance or put them on your phone to refer to when you get there. Be sure to be gracious and appreciative of the invitation.

I might change my mind: Yes, I plan to attend. Please be aware I might change my mind or I might need to leave early. Do not feel bad or take it personally.

Give me time to respond: Thanks for the invite. Is it okay if I take a few days to get back to you about this? If I forget to respond, please remind me. Because of the grief, I'm forgetting a lot of things these days.

I can only stay a few hours: Thanks for the invite. I do plan to attend, but I'll only be able to stay for a few hours. If on that day I feel like staying longer, is it okay if I let you know then?

I'm not ready: Thank you for the invitation, but I'm not ready this year to spend several hours with others celebrating. Be sure to ask me again next year.

Don't try to cheer me up: I know it might be difficult or uncomfortable to be around me right now. Please don't try to cheer me up or try to say something helpful. Please pray for me, and a hug and your presence are all I need.

I may need a room to excuse myself to: I might need to excuse myself to another room if I feel overwhelmed or need to be alone for a period of time. Please let me know in advance which room I could use.

Talk about my loved one: Please don't avoid talking about [my loved one]. Yes, I am sad and I might cry, but it's hurtful when people don't even mention his/her name.

Don't worry if I cry: Please be aware that I might start crying, and that's okay. Tears are part of my life right now, and it's important that I allow myself to grieve.

Thank you for praying and caring: I appreciate your prayers. Thank you for caring.

Don't set me up with anyone: I know you want what you think is best for me, but please don't try to set me up with anyone. It's important for me to focus on my spiritual and emotional health right now.

I'm not having alcohol: I'll just be having soda and water. It's wiser for me to keep my head clear.

Let's plan a visit for a different day: I would love to spend time with you. Would it be okay if we plan a different time to get together when there won't be so many other people around? Are you available on [date/time]?

I'm trying to be honest in my grief: Please understand I am trying to be honest in my grief. That means I will not be putting on a pretend face of holiday cheer. Despite my grief, I am thankful to be surrounded by people who care.

Social event survival

Preparation is key! These ideas can help make it easier for you to attend holiday and social events. Check the ideas you might try:

- ○ Arrive late and/or leave early.
- ○ Attend with someone who will run interference for you and help you interact with people, and who will understand when you're ready to leave. Someone who could come with me: _____
- ○ Remember that during the holidays you might see people you haven't seen in a while. They might not be aware of the death and could ask about your loved one. This is how I can respond: _____
- ○ Identify a place ahead of time where you can go for a while if you're emotionally overwhelmed. Places I can retreat to in the home or building: _____
- ○ Let the event host know you will be there, so he or she can be aware of ways to help you.
- ○ Beforehand, ask people to pray for you while you're at the event. Someone I can ask: _____
- ○ Have someone you can call if you are attending the event alone, and it becomes too much. Someone I can call: _____

Watch video
Hear helpful tips on how to survive the holidays
GRIEFSHARE.ORG/HOLIDAYVIDEO

Controlling negative self-talk when you're alone

Spending time alone during the holidays can be productive, but a danger to avoid and prepare for is negative self-talk, such as: *I can't do this. No one understands. It's all my fault. No one cares.*

To control negative self-talk, you have to counter it with God's truth. Look at how Carla and Robert used the Bible to deal with their negative self-talk:

	Negative self-talk	**God's truth**	**Positive affirmation**
Carla	"No one can relate to this. I'm really alone in this."	• "The LORD is close to the brokenhearted." (Psalm 34:18a) • God says He is with me, and He has given me people in my life who care for me. • "Brothers and sisters, … encourage the disheartened." (1 Thess. 5:14a)	"The truth is, God can equip other people to care for me."
Robert	"Holiday festivities didn't interest me at all. There was nothing to be happy about."	• "You should remember the words of the Lord Jesus: 'It is more blessed to give than to receive.'" (Acts 20:35b NLT)	"Sitting at home doesn't solve anything. But bringing happiness to other folks is more meaningful to me. I will be blessed by helping others."

In your life

- What negative self-talk goes through your mind when you don't rein it in?
- Prayerfully write down a truth from the Bible that can help you rein in this self-talk.

Holiday Journal

Tips for surviving social events

Writing out your hurts and frustrations can help you make sense of your feelings. Write your responses to one or more of the topics below in a separate notebook or journal. Or you could choose to write about a different topic.

- What concerns do you have about attending the different events and get-togethers coming up this season? (You could address each event separately.)
- How do you feel about attending church during the holidays?
- List the safe, uplifting people in your life you'll want to make a point to spend time with this holiday. Describe why you chose each of these people.
- Describe what has been the most difficult part of the holidays so far.

Chapter 4

Surviving Thanksgiving & Christmas Day

Celebrate? That probably is not the word you would use to describe how you feel this holiday season. And there is no way around it: You will be challenged by the usual cheer this time of year. But you can make it through the holidays, and be able to look ahead to the new year, as you find ways to remember and honor your loved one and focus on the true meaning of Christmas.

This chapter helps you understand:

- **Ways to remember and honor your loved one**
- **The importance of moving forward, while remembering**
- **How helping others helps you**
- **What it could mean to be thankful this year**
- **How to use the holidays to look forward in your life**

Survivor Stories

Bekah and Eric began to look at Christmas differently after their losses, finding hope in the true meaning of the holiday.

"At Christmas, we think about Jesus as a little baby and how sweet and innocent that was—and then Easter is when He came to suffer. I realized His whole life was suffering. He was misunderstood, rejected, and laughed at by His own family. And He willingly took that on. When I looked at Christmas that way, it was more beautiful and meaningful than when it was presents and candy."

Bekah

"Acknowledging the birth of Jesus, our Savior, is the reason we're able to experience joy in the midst of our darkest times [see p. 83]. The hope He brings to the world: How can you not celebrate that, having been through what we've been through? Without His sacrifice, we would just be living in a constant state of sadness and have no reason for joy."

Eric

The Strength to *Survive*
Daily Readings

Throughout this season and into the new year, look for opportunities to remember and honor your loved one.

Moving forward— by remembering

God brought you and your loved one together for a period of time and for certain purposes. Preserving memories of that relationship is important for rebuilding your life in a healthy way.

Here are some ways to actively remember your loved one this season:

Talk about your loved one: The holidays provide numerous opportunities to get together and have conversations with people who knew your loved one, which helps preserve memories. Chad Bird, a former pastor who experienced the loss of his adult son and father in the same year, shares how talking about his loved ones with other family members during the holidays was healing:

> There can be a propensity not to talk about those who are no longer there with us for fear of dampening the atmosphere. I think talking about them is healthy. Telling stories about my dad or telling a story about Luke is a way of remembering them, giving thanks for them, and incorporating them into our lives.

Think about (and share) the positive influence: God arranged for you to be influenced by this relationship. Your loved one likely gave you encouragement, advice, affection, or support, and your identity was affected and shaped by his or her example. You can honor your loved one's memory by living out the positive lessons you learned. Consider:

- How did your loved one influence who you've become?
- What positive traits, forged in that relationship, do you want to nurture?
- How might you share these traits with people during the holiday season?

Record special memories: You may find it helpful to keep a record of special memories. You could write them in a journal, book, or blog. You could create a box of keepsakes, put together a photo book, create a T-shirt quilt, or make a video montage.

Contribute to a cause: You can honor your loved one by giving to a worthy cause that touched his or her life. One woman donated teddy bears to a local hospital in honor of her husband, Teddy; another woman volunteered to read to groups of children at the library in honor of her deceased daughter. Ask yourself: "Are there any causes I might contribute to in honor of my loved one?"

These contributions become part of your loved one's legacy.

Cherish the memories

Reflections provides a space to record special memories and lessons learned from your loved one.

- Preserve beloved photos, notes, and mementos.
- Reflect on your relationship.
- Remember your loved one's legacy.

Learn more about this guided journal:
GRIEFSHARE.ORG/JOURNAL

6 signs of healing

Addressing Questions
Working through questions about God and eternity is a sign of healing (see pp. viii–ix).

How Christmas addresses ultimate concerns

After a loved one dies, you will likely have questions about God, heaven, and eternity. A key step toward healing involves resolving questions about ultimate concerns.

You may wonder, *Why did God allow him to die? Could God have prevented her death?* Or, *What happens after we draw our last breath?* God provides important information in the Bible about these matters.

Now, this doesn't necessarily mean getting answers to all your questions. The Bible doesn't provide specific answers to every question you might have about your loved one's death. But what God has revealed to us in the Bible is designed to sustain our faith so we can grow in a relationship with Him.

The meaning of Christmas

The Christmas story is the Bible's fundamental response to the tragedy of death. Everyone will face death, and that is a consequence of a rift between our Creator and us. That rift is due to humankind's sinfulness (rebellion against God). We are separated from God, under God's judgment—and powerless to change that ourselves. However, God has graciously responded to the tragedy of sin and death in a spectacular way. God sent His Son, Jesus, to be born in Bethlehem, to live a life pleasing to God, and to be a sacrifice for us, taking that judgment upon Himself by dying on the cross.

But there's more. Jesus' death was followed by His resurrection. He conquered death! If we trust in Jesus' sacrifice on our behalf, rather than trying to earn God's favor based on our own "merits," then we can look forward to a future resurrection and spending eternity with the Lord. This is why Christmas is a celebration. The birth of Jesus ultimately led to the conquest of death.

"This is how God showed his love among us: He sent his one and only Son into the world that we might live through him." (1 John 4:9)

"For God so loved the world that he gave his one and only Son, that whoever believes in him shall not perish but have eternal life." (John 3:16)

Learn more about God's gift of His Son on pages 83–85.

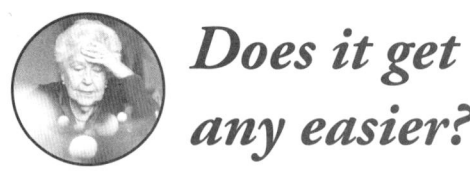
Does it get any easier?

Each holiday after your loved one's death will bring new changes, more memories, and new questions of "Will it be any easier this year?" Be encouraged that it does get easier.

"It may seem like you'll never get through dealing with this loss and pain, but with hard work and God walking alongside you, you will," encourages psychologist Dr. Susan Zonnebelt-Smeenge. She explains that eventually you'll be able to:

- Remember both the positives and negatives associated with your loved one
- Look afresh at what's good in your life right now
- See your new purposes
- Understand how going through difficulty can point us in directions we never would have believed were possible

Words of encouragement
You *will* be able to laugh and enjoy the holidays again. With Jesus, darkness can never overcome you because He has defeated darkness, brokenness, and death (Revelation 21:4). Because of Christ, you can live with hope as you draw closer to Him and come to know Him intimately.

The following are words of encouragement from others who have made it through the darkness to find brighter days ahead:

It will get better: "If I can do it, anyone can. You have to get through those holidays and just reflect back on the memories. You have to go through the valley, but also look forward to future days—because brighter days will be there." – *Jamie, whose wife died*

It does get easier: "It does get easier. You will never get over it, but you will get through it. Some people may take a little longer than others; at each step take the time you need and cry when you need to. Even now, there are times when I'll get choked up, but the tears don't last as long and they're not as hard." – *Brenda, who lost her mom*

Emotional surges will fade: "Eventually, and I cannot tell you how long, but eventually [remembering your loved one] becomes a historical memory. Because you think of something and say, 'Yes, that happened,' but there's not that emotional surge. It's more of a fact. And that tells you that you are moving forward. You are getting there." – *H. Norman Wright, grief and trauma specialist*

"I remember my affliction and my wandering, the bitterness and the gall. … Yet this I call to mind and therefore I have hope: Because of the LORD's great love we are not consumed, for his compassions never fail. They are new every morning; great is your faithfulness." (Lamentations 3:19, 21–23)

Savior God, because of You, I have hope to keep me moving forward, one step at a time. I place my life in Your hands, knowing You are in control and have a perfect plan—a plan that is much bigger than I can comprehend. I trust in You, realizing there is no one like You. Draw me into Your loving arms and empower me to walk forward in this life with You. Amen.

Grief resources
Free videos, articles, and tools for help through grief
GRIEFSHARE.ORG/FREEACCOUNT

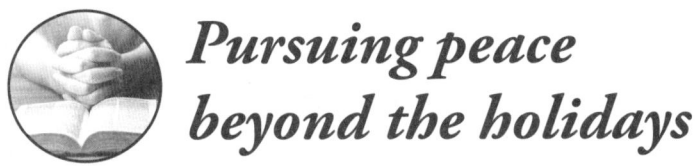

Pursuing peace beyond the holidays

While the holidays can be stressful, finding peace is possible. By reflecting on God and His Word (the Bible), you will draw closer to God, the source of peace. Here's how:

Think what the Bible teaches about God's character and actions

The writer of Psalm 77 cried to God in sorrow and anxiety. But as he poured out his feelings, he started thinking how God had helped him in the past:

"I will remember the deeds of the LORD; … I will consider all your works and meditate on all your mighty deeds." (Psalm 77:11–12)

For example, the Bible teaches that God is faithful, trustworthy, loving, and compassionate (Psalms 18:1–2, 25:10, 33:4, 86:15, 145:5–9).

Read a passage from the Bible and think about the teaching

How can it change and bless you? How can you apply it to your life? Start with this passage:

"Blessed is the one … whose delight is in the law of the LORD, and who meditates on his law day and night. That person is like a tree planted by streams of water, which yields its fruit in season and whose leaf does not wither." (Psalm 1:1–3a)

You could also read from Psalms, Proverbs 10–31, or the book of James.

Record your thoughts about the Bible passage in a journal

If you're not sure what to write, here are some questions as a guide:

- What is the main point in the passage?
- If I applied it, how would my perspective or behaviors change?
- If I don't know how to apply this teaching, who might be able to help me with it?

As you reflect on God's Word consistently, you will gradually begin to notice a difference in the way you think about your circumstances. And that will lead you to enjoy increasing levels of hope and peace.

Redefining hope

Hope probably feels unattainable after loss. In fact, you might wonder what you have left to hope for. But learning the biblical meaning of hope—and realizing it's possible after loss—will shine light on your grief journey and bring comfort in the process.

The biblical meaning of "hope"
When you consider hope, it's easy to slip into our cultural definition of hope as "wishful thinking." However, hope as it's defined in the Bible is holding tightly to the promises of God. God has promised us in His Word that we have eternal life through Jesus' work on the cross (John 3:16). And unlike human promises, which can be broken despite good intentions, God never breaks His promises. As former pastor Randy Alcorn shares, "We have every reason to believe it, and we can bank on it."

Hope means looking toward the future
As pastor Jonathan Pitts shares: "Hope is a joyful expectation of a better tomorrow." But what could such expectations be based on?

Biblical hope is directed toward the future, but it's grounded in God's character. "What is to come actually will come because it's based upon the faithful Lord who has told us what will come," shares former pastor Chad Bird. In other words, we can look to the future in hope, trusting in the Lord's promises because He has been faithful in the past.

In this world we *will* experience pain and suffering. But the story doesn't end there. Biblical hope is knowing that God is good and His future for us is good. Just like a night shadow that vanishes in the morning light, the present pain we're experiencing will one day be replaced by the all-encompassing comfort and peace of eternal life with Christ.

"May the God of hope fill you with all joy and peace as you trust in him, so that you may overflow with hope by the power of the Holy Spirit." (Romans 15:13)

Lord, help me to hold on to Your promises, which are my true source of hope.

6 signs of healing

Sharing Comfort
Comforting and helping others is an indication that you're making progress (see pp. viii–ix).

Reaching out to others

Grief is taxing on you mentally, emotionally, and physically. Yet, ironically, reaching out to help or encourage others helps you. According to author Ron Hutchcraft, whose wife died, "Thinking about others is always going to be part of the healing process."

Here are suggestions you might try on Thanksgiving or Christmas Day (or at any time during the season):

Be intentional and take a chance

Being intentional means thinking in advance about how you can bless someone, even in a small way. This can help energize you to progress through the holidays and beyond. For example, you might consider spending Thanksgiving, Christmas, or New Year's Day with someone who is alone this holiday season. Dr. Albert Hsu, whose father died, reminds us, "The holidays are a time of hospitality, and we can extend the invitation to others who may not have a place to be."

You might invite someone who's experienced a death or a divorce, someone without family nearby, or a nursing home resident. If God puts the thought of a certain person on your heart, don't immediately dismiss that person because you don't think he or she would be interested. Take a chance. You might be pleasantly surprised.*

Volunteer

"I realized," shares Ellie, "the sooner I could get out and volunteer, that helped me a great deal." You might serve a meal at a shelter, visit shut-ins, participate in a toy drive, or make encouraging phone calls.

Help others in your loved one's honor

Karen shares how helping others in her parents' honor was a blessing on her own grief journey: "Because my parents died together, we did a lot of things in their collective memory. We sponsored a [kids' sports] team in their name. We helped redecorate the nursery and preschool rooms in our church … and helped buy a hand-bell set for the church. That would've made them so happy."

"Praise be to the God and Father of our Lord Jesus Christ, the Father of compassion and the God of all comfort, who comforts us in all our troubles, so that we can comfort those in any trouble with the comfort we ourselves receive from God." (2 Corinthians 1:3–4)

God, who needs my help and support? Who is hurting, alone, or in need? Help me look at those around me with new eyes. Help me give Your comfort to other people who are hurting this holiday season. Lead me to them. And give me the courage and energy to follow through.

---

* Remember: Inviting a person of the opposite sex is not wise if you've lost a spouse. A new relationship might be the last thing on your mind, but the other person might think differently. Your healing is of utmost importance; do not jeopardize that.

Moving from an inward to outward focus

Like a turtle who withdraws into its shell in the face of danger, the pain of grief has a way of making you want to retreat inside yourself—especially during the holidays. However, the more you become self-engrossed, the more you remain focused on your own pain and feel physically and mentally worse as a result.

As author and speaker Chad Bird explains, "During the initial phases of grief, there tends to be an inward focus. That's understandable at first. But the longer that I did that, the more unhealthy I became, the more bad decisions that I made, and the worse I became."

God created us for community, and when we look outward and consider how we can serve others instead of looking inward at our own pain, we are living the way God designed us to live—and we find God's comfort in the process. As Chad Bird further shares,

> I ask myself, "How can I take what I've experienced in my life and turn that outward so what I've learned from those experiences can be used in service to the people who are around me?" That was transformational for me because it was so easy just to kind of dwell within myself and close that shell to other people.

While this holiday can make you want to recoil inward, when you resist the temptation to close yourself off from those around you, you create the space for your pain to be transformed into purpose for the good of others.

Reflect

The holidays present a unique opportunity to reach out to those in need. This season, how can you turn your experiences outward in the service of those around you? (For example, this can be as simple as a quick call to check in on someone who's lost a loved one, giving a small gift to a shut-in, or picking up groceries for a busy single mom or someone who doesn't drive.)

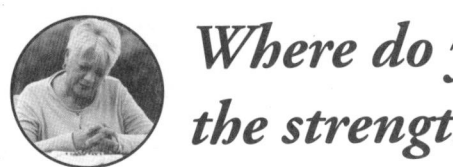

Where do you find the strength?

Moving forward through this season can be draining, but there are ways you can find strength for the journey ahead:

In God's faithfulness

Nora: "August is a particularly difficult month because my first and second husbands *both* died within days of each other in August [of different years]. So August brings with it memories of the loss and the sadness. But now it brings not only those memories, but the realization and the acceptance that God was faithful. He did carry me through that."

In His people

Dr. Paul Tautges: "Romans 12 says that it's good for us to weep with those who weep and to rejoice with those who rejoice. And that's just part of the way God has made us. We really need other people. So intentionally staying in contact was an important part of me working through my grief. I had to have intentional conversations, talking with people about Grandpa and the things we remembered most about him. That was helpful to me."

In thankfulness

Leslie: "The Bible tells us Paul was no stranger to suffering and hardship, and yet he says, 'whatsoever things are good, true, right, and lovely, let your mind dwell on these things.' That takes work to change a channel and go from a negative mindset to a more grateful mindset. But God says when we do, it actually affects our mood, our outlook, and our body."

Shay: "I decided I was going to walk around the lake, and I was going to name everything I was grateful for. So I started walking, and I thanked God for everything: my health, my strength, my right mind, that I can see, that I'm able to walk, the air, the scenery, the trees. The more I said, 'Thank you,' the taller I was standing. I felt like I had strength with each step."

In helping others

Janice: "Sharing with others the hope that I've received in Jesus Christ—the truth that has helped to set me free—has helped me greatly."

Ashley: "Knowing that I could help others really changed me. That's what really allowed my healing to jump into overdrive."

Taking these steps can initially seem difficult, but it's worth the effort. These strength-giving opportunities will help you feel recharged and strengthened for this season and beyond.

Reflect

- Which strength-giving step above resonates with you the most?
- In what ways has God been faithful in your life? What are some things you have to be thankful for? Make a list and meditate on these moments of faithfulness.
- Who can you share laughter, tears, and good conversations with right now?
- Who needs your help right now? And in what ways can you practically help him or her?

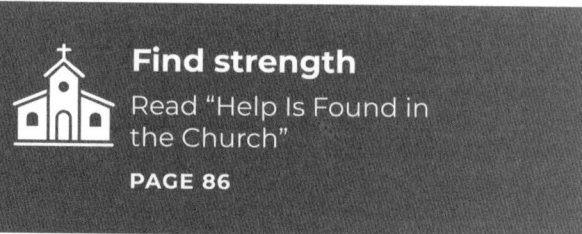

Find strength
Read "Help Is Found in the Church"
PAGE 86

Finding balance this season

Because a loved one will not be present, get-togethers will inevitably feel different—and a wide range of emotions, including sadness, will be part of the experience. While you can cope with these emotions by choosing not to participate in events as much as you did in the past, there is value in spending time with others this season.

Attend the event? Or not this year?

Finding a balance between knowing when to go to holiday get-togethers and when to stay back is one key to emotional health right now. And it might take more than one holiday season to establish a comfortable balance of how you handle each event.

"Being away for Thanksgiving has worked for me [since my wife's death]," shares former pastor Randy Alcorn. "The past two Thanksgivings, I was emotionally not ready to be there with a large number of people. But I don't think I'll be away this year."

Pause hosting the event? And resume later?

Maria shares a similar experience:

> After my mom passed, Thanksgiving and Christmas were not ignored, but we were not getting anyone together. That was probably for the first two years after she passed. After that, we really wanted to. Now, we get everyone in the same house, and everybody brings something to the table, watches movies together, and plays games.

Holiday get-togethers can be healing

When thinking about whether to choose solitude or interaction, it's important to understand that being with others can feel happy and sad at the same time—not only is this okay, but it's also healthy and to be expected. Former pastor Chad Bird, who lost his young adult son and father, shares how his holiday get-togethers with family were emotionally complex yet ultimately healing:

It wasn't as if the days were just terrible and full of pain. There was happiness there; we laughed. But mixed in was also the regret that somebody else was sitting in that chair where Luke always sat. ... Dad wasn't there to tell his stories. But we also know that they were with Christ. They were happy. That knowledge that our loved ones are with Christ in heaven has a way of sending light into the darkest days, whether it's a Thanksgiving or Christmas or some other day of remembrance in which we keenly feel their absence.

Think through in advance how you want to approach events this season, and know that it's okay to change your mind and make adjustments as you go along.

Lord, please give me the wisdom to find balance this season and the grace to be present with my loved ones and my emotions.

Reflect

Asking yourself the following questions can help you find balance this holiday season:

- What event/s do you want to attend this year?
  - How do you think this event might make you feel?
  - How can you prepare emotionally for this event?
- What event/s will you *not* attend this year?
  - What makes you not want to attend this event?
  - What can you do instead?

Not feeling guilty about celebrating

If you choose to attend get-togethers this year, it's important to know that you will experience a wide range of emotions, and you shouldn't feel guilty or embarrassed about how these emotions present themselves.

Dr. Robert DeVries, whose wife died, explains it this way: "At a party, you can be laughing at eight o'clock and crying at eight-thirty because something triggered it. Don't be embarrassed about laughing, because even in the midst of our sorrow there's joy. It's all mixed up together, and it doesn't come in sequence."

If you find yourself enjoying an event or tradition, it's understandable that you might feel guilty, as if your happiness somehow dishonors your loved one. But it's important to fight this response and realize that it's okay—and therapeutic—to laugh and enjoy yourself. And in fact, your loved one would want you to be happy and not feel guilty.

Former pastor Randy Alcorn shares how a friend who lost his 31-year-old son to a drug overdose felt guilty the first time he laughed:

> [He] was having a good time, and he just felt terrible guilt, like, "How could I do this? I'm dishonoring my son." But, no, you're not. One thing I've said to people is "If you're feeling good, thank God you're feeling good. Know that the person you lost would be delighted."

As you decide whether to attend social events and in what ways, remember that it's okay to feel whatever emotion you're experiencing. And it's essential to give yourself the grace to express those feelings however that looks for you.

Lord, I'm thankful for the small windows of laughter amid my pain. Please help me to embrace these moments and not feel guilty.

Reflect

- Have you found yourself feeling guilty for laughing or feeling happy this season? If so, what was the situation?

- How do you think your loved one would want you to feel?

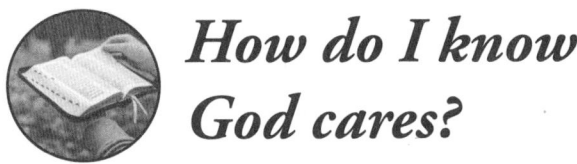
How do I know God cares?

Grief can make you feel alone—and the holidays have a way of making you feel *really* alone. While everyone is busy decorating, enjoying traditions, and being wrapped up in their own lives, you're left feeling isolated on the sidelines with your pain.

It's easy to feel like people are avoiding you or don't have time for you. And even if they do reach out, you may worry that you will dampen their holiday cheer with your sadness and unpredictable emotions.

When your heart cries out for comfort, it's essential to know that God is here, and He intimately understands and empathizes with your pain and grief. While it might be difficult to feel His care when you're hurting so badly, there are ways to be reassured that God is present in your pain—and that He cares about you deeply and eternally.

Author and podcaster Clarissa Moll, whose husband died, shares how she reminds herself of God's care for her:

> When I think about how I know God cares for me, I look to the Bible and the reassurances that He is present with people who are suffering. It says God is near to the brokenhearted: He cares about our tears and keeps them in a bottle because they're so important to him.
>
> The Bible also says Jesus came to be with us and He was the "man of sorrows." He was acquainted with grief. Even when no one else in the whole world understands what it feels like to live inside my grief, Jesus understands. God understands what it's like.

Brenda, whose mom and dad died, feels God's care for her when she remembers how Jesus is personally touched by our grief: "The most comforting thing to me was where it says in the Bible 'Jesus wept.' It's a very heartfelt verse to me, because Jesus saw the family's grief when [His friend] Lazarus passed away. And when He saw their brokenness, He wept. When I read that, I knew He was touched by mine too. He really does care."

Lord, sometimes I feel so alone in my grief and pain. Please help me to feel Your loving arms wrapped around me. Please help me to feel Your care.

The benefits of finding a support group

Do you know the famous image of a man pushing a heavy stone uphill all by himself? This is what it's like attempting to face the holidays alone after loss. However, that burden can be lightened when you find a supportive group of people who understand what you're going through this season.

Other people get what you're going through

Finding a supportive group of people who understand the unique struggles of the holidays after loss will allow you to:

- *Have an idea of what to expect.* Talking to people who've walked this path before you will help you anticipate potential bumps along the way and learn what's worked for them—and what might work for you.

- *Realize you're not alone.* The holidays can feel so lonely, but connecting with people who understand will help you feel supported and encouraged—and also help you resist the urge to isolate.

- *Find supportive friends.* When you're having a particularly difficult day or struggle, having the option to call or to meet with someone who cares is an invaluable way to work through what you're experiencing.

They can help you work through challenges

If you know someone who has navigated the holidays after loss, that person can be instrumental right now as you work through the challenges of the season. It could be a family member, friend, coworker, or even someone you don't know well.

If you already have a close relationship, share how you're feeling and invite the person to share what's worked in his or her situation. If you aren't close already, starting this connection can look like calling the person, sending an email/text/note, or inviting him or her out for coffee or lunch to share your heart and experiences.*

GriefShare groups are available for you to join

A good option is to join a grief support group, like GriefShare, and attend a 2-hour Surviving the Holidays event (both are available in person and online). You'll find a safe, caring space to hear from others who share your experiences.

You can learn more about these support groups here:

- Surviving the Holidays: griefshare.org/holidays
- GriefShare: griefshare.org

"It helped me because I was around a group of people who were grieving themselves. Knowing I was not alone and that these people understood my emotions was such a powerful thing to experience," shares Andrea, who attended a Surviving the Holidays event.

"Finally, brothers and sisters … encourage one another … and the God of love and peace will be with you." (2 Corinthians 13:11)

Lord, it's easy to feel so alone this season. Please help me make meaningful connections that can help me work through the struggles I'm experiencing.

---

* Remember: Inviting a person of the opposite sex may not be wise if you've lost a spouse. A new relationship might be the last thing on your mind, but the other person might think differently. Your healing is of utmost importance, and it's essential not to jeopardize that.

You're not alone.

At a GriefShare group, people understand what you're going through.

Many groups are starting in the new year.
Join one today!

GRIEFSHARE.ORG
Groups meet both in person and online.

Survival Tips

The exercises in this section will help you apply the practical ideas in this book to your own life.

Your loved one's legacy

Part of a person's legacy are the good traits, lessons, deeds, and memories that he or she left with those still living. Your loved one's legacy lives on through you and through all the people your loved one touched in life. The holidays are a nice time to remember and record this legacy.

Write down valuable character traits that your loved one exemplified.

What good lessons have you learned from your loved one?

How will you make a point to pass on those good traits and lessons to other people?

Ideas

- Ask family and friends to write down a special memory and something they learned from your loved one. Compile them into a book to share.

- At family get-togethers, plan to go around the room and share a humorous and happy memory of a time with your loved one. Or have everyone share your loved one's legacy in their lives.

- Start a memory journal. Fill your journal with special memories of times with your loved one. This journal will bring you joy, laughter, and bittersweet tears in the years to come.

- Be sure to tell others that it's okay for them to talk about your loved one in your presence.

Remembering & honoring your loved one

To remember and honor your loved one this season, consider these ideas. Choose one or more that might interest you.

 Plant a tree: Buy a small, live tree to plant in your yard. The tree will be there for years to come and can be decorated with lights each year.

 Hang stockings: You could hang the missing family member's stocking and have people put a little gift, remembrance, or note in it.

 Donate to a cause: If your loved one had a heart for children, animals, nature, etc., volunteer time or money helping an organization in his or her honor.

 Do an art project: Create a scrapbook, photo book or collage, quilt, wood project, garden, Christmas ornament, or something else in his or her honor.

 Display a meaningful item: Set out a special item to remember your loved one (favorite flower, figurine, photo, candle, Christmas cactus, or sports memorabilia).

 Visit the cemetery: Decorate the grave with flowers, a small tree, or a cross.

 Discuss your loved one: Talk about him or her around the dinner table or Christmas tree. Share memories, lessons learned from your loved one, and traits to imitate.

 Cook/bake: If your loved one had a favorite cookie/cake or meal, make that food and give it to a person who would be thankful to receive it.

 Share photos: Have everyone share a special picture of your loved one and the memory associated with that picture.

 Plan a remembrance night: Include other friends who have lost loved ones. Provide ornaments or have people bring one to hang on the tree in remembrance of their loved ones. Invite people to share special Christmas memories.

Be thankful

Thankfulness is a healing tool. Consider what you are grateful for this Thanksgiving and Christmas Day:

> "I'm grateful I had my father for as long as I did, that he was the person he was, and that God had uniquely given him to me."
> – *Phil Sasser, pastor*

> "I'm so grateful Jesus made it possible for me to see my son again one day." – *Hollis*

> "I am grateful for our church and how well they've cared for us."
> – *Carla*

> "I'm grateful to have my family." – *Shay*

What are you thankful for?

Check off what you are thankful for.

- ○ The time I had with my loved one.
- ○ That I'll see my loved one again.
- ○ My loved one is no longer suffering.
- ○ What I've learned from my loved one.
- ○ How God is helping me, comforting me, and providing for me in my grief.
- ○ My family.
- ○ My church.
- ○ My friends.
- ○ Good memories.
- ○ God and His promises.

Write down anything else you are thankful for today.

Helping others helps you

Receiving support and encouragement from others is important. But so is *offering* support and encouragement!

> "One way you can shift your focus off of the pain is to focus on helping other people while you are hurting."
> – Dr. Alfonza Fullwood, pastor

> "I called a lady in our church whose husband had died, and I left her a message. I knew exactly how her heart felt … so empty. After she got home, she called me and said, 'You have no idea what your phone call meant.' When you reach out and help others, it helps your heart heal too." – *Jeannine*

Below is a list of ways to reach out and help other people. Consider which ideas might suit you, and place a mark next to them. These suggestions are just to broaden your thinking of how you could help others. If you are not ready for this right now, that's fine! Tuck the list away and refer to it later.

Call, invite, visit, or send a card/gift to:

○ A homebound person

○ Someone with no family nearby

○ An international university student

○ A single-parent family or a single parent alone this holiday

○ A person in grief

○ A person facing a separation or divorce

○ A family or child in financial need

○ Someone who has comforted you

○ Other idea: _____

Help meet a person's need by:
- ○ Staying with an ill loved one to provide a break for the caregiver
- ○ Offering child care, especially for a single parent
- ○ Doing gardening/yard work
- ○ Doing painting/repairs
- ○ Doing housework
- ○ Providing meals
- ○ Other idea, suited to your skills/strengths: _____

Serve others in need through a local organization:
- ○ Nursing home/assisted living facility
- ○ Volunteering at a walk/run for a cause
- ○ Library/community organizations
- ○ Soup kitchen
- ○ Women's shelter/pregnancy center
- ○ Jail/prison
- ○ Detention home
- ○ Church ministries
- ○ Rescue squad

Pray that God will bring to mind someone who needs you this season. Your church pastor will also have suggestions of people who are alone this holiday season and of places to volunteer.

Make a list of people and their needs, and pray for them:

- _____
- _____
- _____

"Serve one another humbly in love." (Galatians 5:13b)

Evaluate what worked this season

As you move later into the season, or after the holidays are past, it can be helpful to take the time to examine the traditions and events you participated in (or wish you had). This will allow you to think through what worked and why it was meaningful, and what didn't work. Next year you'll have a written record to help you plan ahead and make decisions.

Use this space to reflect on and evaluate this year's traditions and events.

Traditions and events you did this year

What events or traditions have you done so far that you really enjoyed?

What made this event or tradition meaningful? (Answer for each one you listed above.)

Are there any traditions or events that didn't work well?

What in particular was difficult about it? (Answer for each one you listed in the previous question.)

Are there any familiar traditions or events that you didn't do this year but hope to again in the future?

As you think through these questions, it's important to note that it's okay to put familiar traditions or events on the shelf if they feel too painful. You can always try them again another year.

And if you started a new tradition this year, it doesn't mean you have to keep it going. You might instead choose to view it as a "transitional" activity that you put in place for a time, to help you get through.

No matter how the traditions and events went this year, keep in mind that thinking through what works best each holiday season is a process—and checking in with yourself will be essential for making meaningful adjustments in the future.

Holiday Journal

Surviving Thanksgiving & Christmas Day

Use a separate notebook or journal to write out your responses to one or more of the topics below. Remember that your journal is for you; what you record is between you and God.

- Describe your favorite Thanksgiving or Christmas memories of your loved one.

- Name some of your favorite gifts that you received from your loved one. What was the first gift you remember receiving from your loved one? Think about the two most significant gifts: What made them so important to you?

- Read the quote from family counselor Dr. Ramon Presson below. Write your reaction to God being with us and for us.

    "One of the main messages of Christmas is that God not only exists, but He leans in, He cares, and He's involved. Our God is not a distant, detached observer, but God in Christ Jesus, Immanuel, is with us, and He is for us. We're not alone."

Holiday help
Articles and videos for seasonal support
GRIEFSHARE.ORG/HOLIDAYHELP

A Different Kind of Gift

Grief can cast a shadow on the holidays, causing Christmas lights to appear dim, family meals to taste bland, and social gatherings to feel isolating. Perhaps you feel like Amy, whose sister-in-law died:

> *"At Christmas you're supposed to be joyful. But there was no joy in my world and certainly no happy New Year to come."*

When your heart is in this state, you may wish you could hide from the holidays and fast-forward through the pain. But what if the key to finding relief from despair is found in the meaning of Christmas?

A step toward peace

Amy, who did not typically attend church, went to a Christmas Eve service. She was surprised to realize:

"That service was probably one of the first times I actually felt any peace."

While there, Amy saw an ad for a GriefShare group, and she knew she needed to go. The first time she attended, she says:

> *"Unfortunately, I was hungover because of continuing to drown my sorrows with alcohol. So I walked into the church, not knowing if I would be kicked out. What I found, however, was a group of people who welcomed me."*

Permission to grieve

After the first meeting, Amy felt a change inside of her. She learned about giving herself permission to grieve, and that struck a chord. For the first time, she felt hope that this pain might not drive the rest of her life.

> *"Eventually I started to work through my regrets and anger. I worked on forgiving my sister-in-law and receiving forgiveness myself. It was life-changing."*

Amy was introduced to a loving, merciful, and forgiving God:

"God was willing to take all that I had been carrying around, locked up so tight inside of me, and He loved me in spite of it. It was powerful!"

A healing relationship

The more she learned about God from GriefShare, Amy knew she wanted to have a personal relationship with Jesus, God's Son.

What does that mean? A personal relationship with Jesus starts when we recognize we've fallen short of what God expects. We recognize we are what the Bible calls "sinners." Basically that means our thoughts, desires, priorities, and behaviors aren't in line with God's desire for us: to love and honor Him and to always seek the best interests of others.

And God loves us—you!—so much that, even though we deserve judgment for our sinfulness, He made a way for us to escape judgment and avoid the consequences of our sin!

> **For God so loved the world that he gave his one and only Son, that whoever believes in him shall not perish but have eternal life.**
> John 3:16

Receiving God's free gift

The true meaning of Christmas is about God's gift to us: Jesus. Jesus never sinned, and because of His perfect life, He could stand in our place and receive the judgment we deserve.

And He did—by dying on a cross to pay the price for our sins. Then He was raised from the dead, in triumph over sin and death. When we accept Jesus' sacrifice for us, we can receive the forgiveness we desperately need, just like Amy did.

If you recognize your need for Jesus' forgiveness and want to have a life-changing relationship with Him, you can pray something like this:

Dear God, I don't always get everything right. In fact, I have been stubbornly living life on my own terms, and I see how wrong that is. Thank You for sending Jesus to stand in my place and receive the punishment for my sins. Thank You for forgiving me and granting me eternal life with You. Lead me and guide me from this moment forward. Amen.

Your new life with Jesus

Just like the glittering Christmas lights illuminate the darkest winter nights, a relationship with Jesus creates hope in the bleakest circumstances. Vaneetha, whose infant son died, describes it this way:

> *"This life is like wrapping paper. It will get torn; eventually it will be gone. The only thing that will stay is the gift. And that is a new life with Jesus."*

Your new life with Jesus begins when you ask for His forgiveness and receive Him as your Lord and Savior. And just like a seed needs watering and care to bloom, you need the wisdom, guidance, and support of other Christ followers to grow and flourish as a follower of Jesus. You can find this kind of support by attending and getting involved in a local church. Learn more about the benefits of church and what to expect on the next page.

Help Is Found in the Church

Maybe you've found great support and help in your church, or perhaps you've had a bad experience in the past and are hesitant to go into a church. We encourage you to take the step of finding and attending a Bible-focused, Christ-centered church—a place where God's love and compassion is evident.

What kind of church to look for

You'll want to find a church where the Bible is taught, where God's Word is read, studied, explained, and talked about. A place where other Christians will gladly help you find answers to your questions and will support you along the way.

There are many different churches that fulfill these essential criteria, so once you've established that it is a Bible-teaching, Christ-focused church, you can look for other aspects that resonate with you. For instance, some churches are large, while others are small. Some are formal and follow long-standing traditions, while others are more relaxed. Some start early on Sunday morning, while others offer Saturday evening services, and so on.

Small groups within the church

Many churches offer small groups during the week. You might be interested in being in a Bible study, the choir, a grief support group, prayer group, craft group, etc. Find out what's available. Being part of a smaller group keeps you from being "lost in the crowd" on a busy Sunday morning. It's a great way to build friendships, develop a support system, and learn more about God's plans, His promises, and His love for you.

Where to start in finding a church

A good starting place to find the right church for you is to do a search online for churches in your area. Typically, a church will include their "statement of faith" or "mission statement" that tells you the essentials about what the church believes. This will help you determine if the church is Bible-focused and Christ-centered.*

The next step is to attend a church service to get a feel for the way the service is run and the people who go there. If you feel welcomed and the preaching is sound (in accordance with God's Word, the Bible), this might be a good fit! It's important to note that many churches offer online services, which can be another way to get a feel for the church if you can't attend in person.

Once you're committed to a church, you'll want to get connected in deeper ways, so be sure to ask church leadership about small-group or Bible study opportunities.

---

* This book is associated with the GriefShare ministry organization. Read our statement of faith at griefshare.org/beliefs.

Surviving the Holidays

Event Tools

If you're at a Surviving the Holidays event, welcome! (If you're reading this guide outside of an event and would like to learn more about attending, visit griefshare.org/holidays.)

In this section you'll find materials for use during and after the event:

- **What to expect today**
- **What if I'm not sure about God?**
- **Video note-taking outline**
- **Meet the experts and people who shared their stories**
- **Take inventory**
- **GriefShare resources for help on your grief journey**

What to Expect Today

The holiday season is here, and with it comes a focus on family, traditions, social events, and cheer—all of which can cause difficult emotions to surface. And this is likely why you're here. Whether this is the first, second, or tenth holiday after your loved one's death, the emotions that may arise in the days ahead can blindside you.

With Surviving the Holidays, you'll be better prepared for what's to come and can approach the season with a sense of calm and assurance. You'll find support and direction to navigate the holidays in a healthy way.

3 essential parts of Surviving the Holidays

Video
You'll hear helpful guidance from grief recovery experts and people who've faced personal loss, who discuss:

- How to prepare for hard-hitting emotions
- What to do about yearly traditions
- Ways to handle social events
- Where to find comfort, strength, and hope

A video outline for taking notes is on pp. 92–93. You can access the video online at **griefshare.org/holidayvideo**.

Discussion
You'll have the chance to talk with others about what you learned from the video. There's no pressure to share if you don't want to, but you can benefit from listening.

Personal reflections
This guide has practical strategies, encouragement, tips, and exercises. Commit to reading one or two pages daily. You are welcome to skip around the book.

Find articles and video clips at **griefshare.org/holidayhelp**.

What If I'm Not Sure About *God?*

Y ou're here today because you've experienced the death of someone close. Now, Surviving the Holidays is a Christian program, based on the Bible's teaching—and, honestly, you might not be sure what you think of God right now. You might even be angry with God, wondering why He didn't stop what your loved one went through that ended in his or her death. These feelings and questions are understandable, and it's helpful to be honest about such struggles.

Some of your questions and feelings are probably addressed in the video and in this guide, because people in the Bible also had the same questions, concerns, and complaints. So, when we refer to passages in the Bible, we ask only that you consider what you might learn from others whose grief challenged their faith.

Surviving the Holidays is a special holiday seminar produced by GriefShare, a grief support group program. We encourage you to find and attend a GriefShare group (**griefshare.org**); you will be glad you did.

Grief resources
Free videos, articles, and tools for help through grief
GRIEFSHARE.ORG/FREEACCOUNT

Video Outline

Write down important points you'd like to remember, or questions you may have, while viewing the video.

Challenging days ahead

Preparing for the holidays

Plan ahead

Consider your traditions

Responding to invitations

Getting through the day

Face the pain

Remember your loved one

Learning from the holidays

Thanksgiving

Christmas

Hear helpful tips on how to survive the holidays
GRIEFSHARE.ORG/HOLIDAYVIDEO

Meet the Experts

Video cohosts

David and Nancy Guthrie faced the deaths of two children. They minister to others in grief through Respite Retreats, speaking, and writing. Their books include *When Your Family's Lost a Loved One*, *Holding On to Hope*, and *Hearing Jesus Speak into Your Sorrow*. The Guthries also cohost the 13-week GriefShare program videos.

Expert insights

These are some of the featured experts in the Survival Guide and the video.

Randy Alcorn
Author and former pastor; his wife and mom died

Chad Bird
Author and podcaster; lost his young adult son and father

Sabrina D. Black
Counselor and author; experienced death of multiple relatives and a miscarriage

Cindy Bultema
Author and speaker; fiance died in a workplace accident

Dr. Kathryn Butler
Trauma surgeon and author; lost a close friend

Dr. Tate Cockrell
Professor and counselor; brother died

Dr. Zoricelis Davila
Psychotherapist and professor; parents and close friend died

Ron Deal
Marriage and family therapist, author; son passed away at age 12 from MRSA

Dr. Robert DeVries
Author and retired pastor; first wife died of cancer

Mel Erickson
Author and grief educator; son died

Dr. Alfonza Fullwood
Pastor and professor

Dr. Brad Hambrick
Counselor and pastor; grandfather died

Dr. Albert Hsu
Author and editor; lost his father to suicide

Ron Hutchcraft
Speaker and author; wife died

Omar King
Counselor; mother died

Susan Lutz
Counselor and author; mom died of heart attack, dad died of lung cancer

Dr. Elias Moitinho
Counselor and professor

Clarissa Moll
Podcaster and author; husband died during a hiking accident

Meet the Experts

Jonathan Pitts
Pastor and author; wife died

Dr. Ramon Presson
Marriage and family therapist, author

Lois Rabey
Author and speaker; husband died from a hot-air balloon accident

Robert Rogers
Author and speaker; wife and four children drowned in a flash flood

Phil Sasser
Pastor; father died from complications due to emphysema

Dr. Paul Tautges
Pastor and counselor; parents and granddaughter died, uncle was murdered

Dr. Paul David Tripp
Counselor and author; lost his father

Leslie Vernick
Relationship coach and author

H. Norman Wright
Grief and trauma expert, author; wife and son died

Dr. Susan Zonnebelt-Smeenge
Psychologist and author; husband died 18 years after being diagnosed with a brain tumor

Meet Those Who Shared Their Stories

These people bravely shared their stories to help others, like you, find hope and support on the grief journey.

Amy
Sister-in-law died from alcohol abuse

Ashley
Father-in-law died from heart failure

Bekah
Husband died from an unknown cause

Bill
Wife died from a stroke

Brenda
Mom and dad died

Carol
Husband died from cancer

Carla
Husband died from a blood clot to his heart

Connie
Mom died

Ellie
Two husbands died from cancer

Eric
Daughter died from cancer

Heather
Sister died from cancer

Hollis
Son died from a heart condition

 **Janice**
Brother died by suicide; parents died

 **Jason**
Mother died

 **Jamie**
Wife died from a brain aneurysm

 **Jeannine**
Husband died from surgical complications

 **Jemma**
Sister died in a car accident

 **JoAnne**
Husband died from cancer

 **Karen**
Parents died in a plane accident

 **Mardie**
Husband died

 **Maria**
Mom died

 **Marilyn**
Husband died from a rare cancer

 **Marion**
Husband died from a stroke

 **Mike**
Wife died from a medical issue

 **Nora**
First child was stillborn; two husbands have died

 **Robert**
Multiple family members died

Scott
Wife died from cancer

Shay
Mother died from cancer

Sheila
Husband died from cancer

Tom
Father died from a heart attack and mother died from cancer

Vaneetha
Multiple miscarriages and the death of her infant son due to a doctor's error

Willie
Wife died from heart failure

Meet Those Who Shared Their Stories

Take inventory

Now that you've experienced the Surviving the Holidays event, it would be a good idea to think about how you might use what you've learned.

- *List the three most important ideas you've heard from the Surviving the Holidays program.*

- *What practical suggestions will you try out?*

- *How has your perspective about the holiday season changed as a result of what you heard today?*

Find support
at a GriefShare group
GRIEFSHARE.ORG

About GriefShare

Need help dealing with grief? At a 13-week GriefShare support group, you'll find relief, strength, and guidance as you navigate the journey of grief.

At GriefShare, you don't have to have it all together. The people there understand the raw emotions, mental fog, and daily struggles. They won't try to rush you or judge you.

This group offers a safe place where you can express your emotions, or choose to sit quietly and process what you're learning. You'll find out:

- What's "normal" in your grief
- How to handle difficult emotions
- Where to find the strength to go on

The group experience: Each week you'll watch a video with expert counsel and personal stories, spend time in a group discussion (you don't have to talk!), and take home a book for further help on issues you're facing.

Going to a GriefShare group may be one of the best decisions you'll make as you seek to find relief, stability, and peace of mind through the pain of grief.

Find a GriefShare group: **griefshare.org**, **800-395-5755**, **919-562-2112** intl.

"Through GriefShare, you will slowly but surely experience healing."

Donna

GriefShare Resources

GriefShare support groups
Need help dealing with grief? Groups meet in person and online. Visit **griefshare.org**

Surviving the Holidays event
A 2-hour event to help you manage the season. Visit **griefshare.org/holidays**

Free GriefShare account
Access videos and articles for help in navigating your grief at **griefshare.org/freeaccount**

Daily email messages – Free
Receive an encouraging email message every day for a year. **griefshare.org/dailyemails**

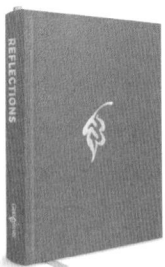

Reflections: A Guided Journal by GriefShare
Experience new ways to journal to find relief and restored stability.
griefshare.org /journal

Grieving with Hope book
Determine whether you're grieving in a way that leads to hope and healing.
griefshare.org /hope

Through a Season of Grief book
These 365 short devotions will help you adjust after loss.
griefshare.org /devotional